Signs of Change

Signs of Change

New Directions in
Secondary Theatre Education

Joan Lazarus
Foreword by JoBeth Gonzalez

HEINEMANN
Portsmouth, NH

Heinemann

A division of Reed Elsevier Inc.
361 Hanover Street
Portsmouth, NH 03801–3912
www.heinemanndrama.com

Offices and agents throughout the world

The names of all students in this book have been changed to protect their privacy.

The author and publisher wish to thank those who have generously given permission to
reprint borrowed material:

Excerpt and Figure 2–3 adapted from *Children as Fellow Citizens: Participation and Commitment* by Micha De Winter. Copyright © 1997 by Micha De Winter. Published by
Radcliffe Medical Press, Ltd. Reprinted by permission of the publisher.

Excerpts from *Discipline-Based Theatre and Education: A Conceptual Framework for Teaching
and Learning Theatre.* Copyright © 1996 by the Southeast Center for Education in the Arts,
University of Tennessee, Chattanooga. Published by the SCEA. Reprinted by permission
of the publisher.

Figures 1–4, 2–5, 2–6, 2–7, 3–3, and 7–1: Photographs of students at Bradford High
School, courtesy of Tom Stanfield.

Figure 2–1: Graphic from McCallum High School Theatre program for *The Diary of Anne
Frank*. Reprinted by permission of Kelley Toombs, Kelley Toombs Design.

Credits continue on page vi

Library of Congress Cataloging-in-Publication Data
Lazarus, Joan.
    Signs of change : new directions in secondary theatre education / Joan Lazarus.
        p. cm.
    Includes bibliographical references and index.
    ISBN 0-325-00490-0 (alk. paper)
    1. Theater—Study and teaching (Secondary) I. Title.

PN2075.L36 2004
372.66—dc22   2004007822

Editor: Lisa A. Barnett
Production: Lynne Reed
Cover design: Jenny Jensen Greenleaf
Compositor: Valerie Levy/Drawing Board Studios
Manufacturing: Steve Bernier

Printed in the United States of America on acid-free paper
08   07   06   05   04   EB   1   2   3   4   5

I have such a yearning for the future. It is boundless!
Eric Overmyer, *On the Verge*

This book is dedicated to my son, Michael—the light of my life;
and to my students—the hope for our future.

Credits continued from page iv

CONTENTS

FOREWORD

Even educational institutions, often slow or resistant to change—holding
steadfast to tradition—undergo transformation. In *Signs of Change: New
Directions in Secondary Theatre Education*, Joan Lazarus gives us a glimpse of
some change makers in secondary school theatre education. For them, change is
sometimes an exhilarating adventure, sometimes an intimidating trial. They are
teachers who create and promote different and dynamic theatre programs, often
within institutions that perceive theatre as mainstream, conventional, and structured by decades-old pedagogies.

Programs that nurture fresh perspectives require teachers to experiment with
the shape, form, and content of their pedagogy. If change requires experimentation, how do we build a bridge long and stable enough for both experienced and
new teachers to cross from tradition to experimentation? *Signs of Change* is a part
of that bridge.

Joan Lazarus compiles and synthesizes the voices of teachers across the United
States whose teaching and directing displaces common perceptions of theatre
education. She captures with sensitive clarity the struggles inherent to teachers
whose risks are changing the face of theatre education. From them we learn that
interrogating our own practice is necessary to sustaining the vitality of our programs. Much of what we discover about ourselves and about theatre occurs when
we are confident enough to say to students, "I don't know. Let's find out together." *Signs of Change* offers suggestions for encouraging students to contem-
plate critical issues, involving students as coartists, and including students who
represent marginalized components of a school. Joan's emphasis on socially responsible theatre teaching and student-centered learning points to the kind of
change in theatre teaching that can make significant shifts in the way we practice
the art of teaching theatre.

This book fills a great void in theatre education literature because it com-
prises our colleagues' voices. In this unique and substantial resource, Joan orga-
nizes and connects discussions of theatre education philosophies, descriptions

of detailed activities, and stories of risk taking, all of which define innovative approaches to teaching theatre. Joan introduces companions who will encourage you to forge ahead with your instincts, even though your instincts may contradict the traditions of your training or your institution's expectations to maintain the norm.

Signs of Change represents a journey for Joan of which I have had the privilege to be a part. With Joan's crucial leadership, and support from professional organizations and many colleagues, Joan and I have launched think tanks on theatre education reform at conferences from New York to San Diego. Over late-night long-distance telephone conversations, in hotel rooms and lobbies, and in the think tanks themselves, I have observed the questions emerge that are central to this book: What is "best practice," and what does best practice look like in theatre classrooms and rehearsals? How do classrooms and rehearsals operate when the student is at the center of the learning process? What does it mean to be a "socially responsible" teacher or student? *Signs of Change* reflects Joan's long-term commitment to theatre teachers whose innovative strategies transfigure theatre education.

The fundamental shift into this transfigured practice requires teacher-directors and students to negotiate new and contingent relationships. The traditional secondary school theatre director is the decision maker who is driven by deadlines, maintains the through-line of the play, and orchestrates teams of young artists and technicians. When teachers relinquish the expected role of authority in favor of a student-centered methodology, the risks increase: we may send cross signals to our students, fear administrative condemnation, and lose confidence. Nevertheless, the rewards of a student-centered and socially responsible theatre program are immense.

Signs of Change: New Directions in Secondary Theatre Education is both stimulating and validating. If you are soon to enter the field, the models presented here may inspire you to experiment with an idea that "goes against the grain." If you are a veteran teacher, you may see your own practice resonate with those of your colleagues whose work Joan documents in this book, and you will gain fresh insight. Change happens one teacher, one classroom, and one production at a time. Together, we will change secondary school theatre education to render students as responsible agents who will practice the art and craft of theatre in ways that will prepare them for life.

—*JoBeth Gonzalez*

PREFACE

A Yearning for Change

I have been wondering a lot about change: how it happens, why it happens, and how I can contribute to the positive change I desire for my field. I am inspired and intrigued in my quest for change by the more than one hundred theatre teachers, artists, arts administrators, college professors, and students who were interviewed for this book. All were recommended to me by colleagues, students, coteachers, or professional organizations. Some of the interviewees I knew well or had heard of; some were fresh acquaintances whose work was new to me. I met many of them as strangers and parted from them feeling a bond, a shared passion, as people moving together with eyes fixed on a common goal.

Each of these teacher-artists has embraced change in a unique way and has evolved highly effective practices for teaching and producing theatre with young people. As the author of this book, I am like the child on a summer evening who tries to capture all the fireflies she can in an attempt to illumine the whole backyard. I am the gatherer, the one trying to capture the ephemeral nature of others' work. I hope that the teachers, future teachers, and artists who read *Signs of Change* find some light in these pages, some inspiration and practical ideas to help them embrace change and ensure a promising future for our field.

This book is an invitation to eavesdrop on conversations with a small group of successful teacher-artists who work with young people in dynamic and compelling ways. It has been both a joy and a challenge to write a book like this. The joy comes from the opportunity to talk at length with dedicated professionals who are passionate about theatre with secondary school students. This research has been a blissful opportunity to dream with and learn from remarkable people. The challenge comes from trying to capture in so few words a collection of insights and experiences that are broad, rich, diverse, and are redefining theatre with adolescents. As is also the case with gifted teacher-artists, their work, which is often intuitive and spontaneous, rarely exists in notes, plans, or other documented forms. To capture the passion and potency of their various approaches, I include interview excerpts from the teacher-artists themselves, highlight recurring themes, and share individual and composite stories and lessons related to some of the most effective aspects of their practice. Quotes from other published writers appear within and around the text as a backdrop, counterpoint, and partner in the conversations. All together, the book is both a celebration of advances in the field and a call for change and action. It is a record of multiple versions of the best of what is possible in secondary school theatre education today.

It is important here to note what this book is not. It is not a comprehensive and definitive look at secondary school theatre education in the twentieth or twenty-first centuries nor is it a step-by-step road map to best practice. Critical and theoretical works—as well as methods texts and anthologies on so vast a subject—remain for others to do.

I have been privileged to be, in essence, a conduit between these theatre education professionals and their present and future counterparts around the country. Some readers will find that the ideas and practices in this book resonate with what they already do. I hope these people will find affirmation and encouragement in this book. Others will find inspiration and practical strategies to bring to life their long-held convictions about the power of theatre to change the lives of our children. Still others will find territory unfamiliar and uncomfortable as they compare their current practice to that explored in these pages. May all of us glean from the voices in this book the wisdom, courage, and good humor that make true change possible.

ACKNOWLEDGMENTS

Without the steadfast support and encouragement of my colleagues at The University of Texas at Austin; Sharon Grady, Coleman Jennings, and Suzan Zeder, this book would not have been completed. The research for this book has been possible because of the generous support of the Vice President for Research, the College of Fine Arts and the Department of Theatre and Dance at The University of Texas. Many thanks also are due to my colleagues around the country who recommended teachers and artists to interview and who read drafts of this book as it was being written. Great gratitude is due to Cheryl Green, research assistant, proofreader, and transcription wizard, and to Lara Greene and Scott Tatum for their help with this project.

I am grateful to the many mentors and friends who afforded me inspiration for this project through their example: Wayne Brabender, Susan diRende, Don Doyle, Anne Elgood, Jodie Flint, Kris Fiuty, JoBeth Gonzalez, Bruce Jordan, Jean Stark Hebenstreit, Rhoda Kittelson, Debbie Kyle, Mary Beth Lang, Michelle Pullen, Chuck Quittner, Cynthia Sampson, Roxanne Schroeder-Arce, Laurel Serleth, Kim Wheetley, Elizabeth Wilson, Sue Wood, Lyn Wright, and the Women of Velocity. I am also grateful to family and friends who have taught me, encouraged me, and supported me over the years.

I probably have been best equipped for this journey by students I have had the privilege of working with at Newcastle High School, Nickerson High School, Lincoln High School, various youth theatre programs, the University of Wisconsin–Madison, and The University of Texas at Austin. Each has enriched me by their ideas, questions, and especially by the challenges they presented.

I am indebted to those who granted me an interview, shared their materials, and offered their generous assistance with this project. These people give me hope for the future of this field.

Abigail Adams, People's Light and Theatre Company, Malvern, Pennsylvania

Tara Affolter, East High School, Madison, Wisconsin

Deb Alexander, Bailey Middle School, Austin, Texas

Dave Barnes, Oswego High School, Oswego, Illinois

Donna Barnes, Oswego High School, Oswego, Illinois

Gretta Berghammer, University of Northern Iowa, Cedar Rapids, Iowa

Steve Bogart, Lexington High School, Lexington, Massachusetts

Amy Burtaine, Austin Waldorf School, Austin, Texas

Carol Cain, West Side Magnet School, LaGrange, Georgia

Ben Cameron, Theatre Communications Group, New York, New York

Autumn Samsula Casey, Plano Senior High School, Plano, Texas

Jennifer Chapman, University of Wisconsin–Madison, Madison, Wisconsin

Gloria Bond Clunie, Chute Middle School and Victory Gardens Theatre, Chicago, Illinois

Bob Colby, Emerson College, Boston, Massachusetts

Joanna Cortright, Perpich Center for Arts Education, St. Paul, Minnesota

Bryar Cougle, Department of Public Instruction, North Carolina

Barbara Cox, Perpich Center for Arts Education, St. Paul, Minnesota

Russell Davis, People's Light and Theatre Company, Malvern, Pennsylvania

Sandra DiMartino, Lexington High School, Lexington, Massachusetts

Susan diRende, Teaching Artist, Los Angeles, California

Dave Dynak, Department of Theatre, University of Utah, Salt Lake City, Utah

Gillian Eaton, Teaching Artist, Detroit, Michigan

Jason Ewing, Kingsley School, Evanston, Illinois

Rick Garcia, Johnston High School, Austin, Texas

Carlen Gilseth, Woodlands High School, The Woodlands, Texas

JoBeth Gonzalez, Bowling Green High School, Bowling Green, Ohio

Fursey Gotuaco, Richland Hills High School, North Richland Hills, Texas

Jennifer Gotuaco, Smithfield Middle School, North Richland Hills, Texas

Benjamin Gooding, The University of Texas at Austin, Texas

Maxine Greene, Columbia University Emeritus, New York

Chris Griffith, Galumph Theatre, Minneapolis, Minnesota

Brian Hall, Mountainside Middle School/Saguaro High School, Scottsdale, Arizona

Bill Hansen, Lincoln High School, Manitowoc, Wisconsin

Rebecca Harding, Small Middle School, retired; Austin, Texas

Andrew Harris, Stage One, Louisville, Kentucky

John Heinemann, Lincoln High School, Lincoln, Nebraska

J. Daniel Herring, Stage One, Louisville, Kentucky

Karen Kay Husted, Douglas, Arizona

Jeanne Jackson, Conroe, Texas

Rebecca Jallings, West High School, Madison, Wisconsin

Justine Johnston, Crete, Nebraska

Steven Jones, Stage One, Louisville, Kentucky

Daniel Kelin, Honolulu Theatre for Youth, Honolulu, Hawaii

Sarah Kent, Manor High School, Manor, Texas

Aline Knighton, Crockett High School, Austin, Texas

Patsy Koch Johns, Lincoln High School, Lincoln, Nebraska

Kris Kissel, Sabino High School, Tuscon, Arizona

Kati Koerner, Lincoln Center, New York

Valerie Roberts Labonski, Morton West High School, Berwyn, Illinois

Linda Leedberg, Des Moines, Iowa

Jeffrey Leptak-Moreau, Educational Theatre Association, Cincinnati, Ohio

Brianna Lindahl, Thunder Ridge Middle School, Centennial, Colorado

Jenny Lutringer, Richland Hills High School, North Richland Hills, Texas

Jan Mandell, St. Paul Central High School, St. Paul, Minnesota

Laura McCammon, University of Arizona, Tucson, Arizona

Jean McCullough, Bowling Green High School, Bowling Green, Ohio

Gillian McNally, People's Light and Theatre Company, Malvern, Pennsylvania

Susan Morrell, Cactus High School, Glendale, Arizona

Bethany Nelson, Emerson College, Boston, Massachusetts

David O'Fallon, McPhail Center for the Arts, Minneapolis, Minnesota

Tory Peterson, Perpich High School for the Arts, St. Paul, Minnesota

Rebecca Podsednik, The University of Texas at Austin, Austin, Texas

Nancy Prince, Thomas J. Rusk Middle School, Nacogdoches, Texas

Sue Scarborough, Enloe High School, Raleigh, North Carolina

Rebecca Schlomann, The University of Texas at Austin, Texas

Roxanne Schroeder-Arce, McCallum High School, Austin, Texas

Nancy Shaw, People's Light and Theatre Company, Malvern, Pennsylvania

Dan Seaman, Weaver High School, Greensboro, North Carolina

Kent Seidel, University of Cincinnati, Cincinnati, Ohio

Laurel Serleth, Washington School, Evanston, Illinois

Kent Sorensen, Marana High School, Marana, Arizona

Jerry Smith, Salem High School, Conyers, Georgia

Debbie Spink, Washougal High School, Washougal, Washington

Holly Stanfield, Bradford High School, Kenosha, Wisconsin

Diane Stewart, Cypress High School, Fort Myers, Florida

Wendy Jo Strom, Winterhaven School, Portland, Oregon

Theatre students, Bowling Green High School, Bowling Green, Ohio

Misty Valenta, The University of Texas at Austin, Texas

Chris Vine, Creative Arts Team, New York, New York

Bill Ward, Flint Youth Theatre, Flint, Michigan

Kim Wheetley, Southeast Center for Education in the Arts, Chattanooga, Tennessee

Helen White, Creative Arts Team, New York, New York

Nancy Wilkinson, Peninsula High School, Gig Harbor, Washington

Sue Wood, Flint, Michigan

Youth cast members and staff, . . . *My Soul to Take*, Flint Youth Theatre, Flint, Michigan

Youth Members, Creative Arts Team Youth Theatre, New York, New York

Youth participants and staff, People's Light and Theatre Company, Malvern, Pennsylvania

Sandi Zielinski, Illinois State University, Bloomington, Illinois

Lynda Zimmerman, Creative Arts Team, New York, New York

The author wishes to thank Lisa Barnett, Lynne Reed, and the staff at Heinemann for their encouragement and support of this project.

1

Signs of Change and the Need for Change

The engaged voice must never be fixed and absolute but always changing, always evolving in dialogue with a world beyond itself.

—BELL HOOKS

The world we have made as a result of the level of thinking we have done thus far creates problems we cannot solve at the same level of thinking at which we created them.

—ALBERT EINSTEIN

I think I have been writing this book my whole life. From as early as I can remember I wanted to be a teacher. I wanted to change the world, to make the world better. I also was enthralled by theatre and its power to capture and convey feelings and ideas as big and powerful as my feelings and ideas seemed to be. Now, years after I began teaching, I still yearn for change in theatre and education.

This book explores the convergence of a passion for teaching and a love of theatre as it bears upon the education of young people in middle school and high school. It is a collection of effective practices used by a small but growing number of veteran and novice educator-artists who are passionate about their work. Though the perspectives of professional theatre artists, administrators, students, scholars, and university theatre education professors are included, the voices in this book are primarily those of middle school and high school theatre teachers.

Each of these professionals works at the intersection of artmaking and education, of process and product, of knowing and doing, of teaching and learning. They are in the business of bringing about change in the lives of individual students as well as in their schools and communities. They are pioneers evolving their practice of theatre education in their own frontiers of change, their classrooms.

This book is but a glimpse of the imaginative, forward-looking work being undertaken by dynamic theatre teachers in urban, rural, and suburban settings throughout the country. I welcome you as another pioneer moving toward a new, or perhaps, recycled, practice of theatre education.

Change

Change of any kind—moving, switching jobs, losing a family member—is fraught with a wide range of emotions. There are many reasons I continue to be catapulted into change as a theatre educator. Sometimes I change to accommodate new mandates or initiatives, shifts in programmatic thrust, changes in administration or facilities, or a reduction of funding. Often, I change because of some restlessness or dissatisfaction I feel in my work or just from the desire for something new, something better. One thing I am learning is that whatever the catalyst for change, I have some choices:

- I can hang on to my old views and behaviors, determined that if I just work harder and better surely all will be well and change won't come.

- I can go into denial that a problem exists or that change is needed or imminent.

- I can reflect on my views and practices and actively recycle them into something new.

Just talking and thinking about change makes me take stock of my present situation, a thing rarely easy or comfortable to do. Inspired by the work of David Cooperrider, I know that a look at *what is* brings with it the realization of *what isn't*, that my vision isn't yet my reality. If I try to envision *what might be* and *what ought to be,* I get wildly enthusiastic, but then face fears of *what may never be* (Cooperrider and Whitney 1999; Cooperrider, Sorensen, Whitney, and Yaeger 2000). I sometimes get myself stuck in a cycle of denial, ambivalence, hope, and fear. Whether I initiate change or it is imposed, if positive change is to occur, I must take action that may be at once hard, thrilling, risky, or daunting.

I encountered many changes during my years teaching high school theatre. In one school, I had more than one hundred students involved in the thriving program, which included theatre classes, productions, touring plays for young audiences, a group doing drama in the preschools, a Thespian troupe, and various other performing entities and enterprises. Although I was insanely busy at school every day from before sunup until well after sundown, I felt restless, as though there was more, or something different, I could do or should do to reach students more effectively.

I attended conferences and learned what I could, believing the problem was in what I didn't know and that the elusive solutions were "out there" for me to discover. I found my way to a graduate program that helped me expand and investigate a new range of approaches and techniques. It was when I implemented that learning with my students that I saw fundamental and enduring change begin to take place in my teaching and directing practice. I began adapting, exploring, experimenting, and making these new approaches my own. I allowed myself to make mistakes, to not know, to learn *with* my students. Thus began my present journey, one in which I am learning how to embrace change. My long-held passion for teaching and theatre is now being grounded in my day-to-day practice.

Change and Education

In the pages that follow, I consider the state of theatre education, the need for change to ensure a future for the field, and the emergence of best practice. Before looking at these aspects of our work, it is helpful to examine a broader context for the challenges and opportunities we in theatre education presently face. This requires an honest look at the present state of our schools and a backward glance at what shaped our current educational system.

The changes in my personal teaching practices began amid the rush of reform movements in the 1980s and 1990s. I have heard that change accelerates at the close of each century, and this was certainly true one hundred years ago as the world moved from the nineteenth to the twentieth century. It's amazing to consider how rapid those changes really were and how significant an impact they had: Farm families lost children to big-city factories; People from around the world moved to the United States; More women began working outside of the home and in jobs previously reserved for men. With the advent of child labor laws and mandatory education, a space between childhood and adulthood was created and adolescence emerged. Where and how people lived, worked, communicated, and traveled changed in a relatively short span of time.

These changes rolled and rippled through the remainder of the century. They led to the revolutions in technology and information that today affect how we live, work, and interact in our homes, with family, and in our local and global communities. In addition to the enormous benefits we receive from twenty-first-century advances and conveniences, we have been left with some "hazardous debris" from the twentieth century. Poverty, discrimination, disenfranchised youth, dysfunctional families, failing communities, faltering public institutions, and corrupt private enterprises, while not entirely new to this century, are also part of the legacy of change.

I find it ironic that while we move ever faster in search of better and more efficient material goods and services, much of our thinking remains stuck in early twentieth-century models. This is most apparent in public schools where, despite the trappings of reform, thinking is fixed in a "schools as factories" or "schooling machine" model of education. That entrenched thinking has a direct impact on how theatre typically is taught in our schools.

When and why did this view of education take hold? At the beginning of the twentieth century, public schools were reformed to prepare factory workers for the emerging Industrial Revolution. Students learned how to follow directions, repeat tasks, and be responsible citizens. Now, at the beginning of the twenty-first century, many schools are still using that same model when in fact the world needs creative thinkers and independent, innovative problem-solvers. While our schools have embraced technology and various educational reform strategies, these so-called advances haven't procured the hoped-for panacea, but rather short-term and spotty relief from the systemic problems embedded nearly one hundred years ago. Many twentieth-century reform efforts continue to think of schools as machines with various broken parts. Each tries to fix what's "broken," be it the teachers, students, curriculum, standards, buildings, equipment, or textbooks. Truly effective change occurs only when there is a fundamental change in the way educators think about teaching and learning.

David O'Fallon[1] has been active as a theatre teacher, scholar, arts education advocate, and arts activist for decades. As he reflects on the state of education today, he calls for major shifts in our thinking and practices. David is concerned that the old educational models place little emphasis on learning requiring imagination. He alerts us to the dangers of schools structured in much the same way as in the 1920s, when his mother was a young teacher.

> She taught a school year of about one hundred seventy or so instructional days, with a six- or seven-period day. . . . That is still just about the [current] length of the school year and the school day. . . . It's the same-size box that we had seventy-five years ago, and we're . . . trying to stuff more and more . . . into that box. And it's exploding.
>
> In these extremely crowded, Industrial-model schools, there's hardly any room left for the imagination. . . . We need some profound transformation of how we think. . . . We are at the end of the Industrial Age of education. (O'Fallon 2002)

Zemelman, Daniels, and Hyde concur. They highlight the futility of repeatedly using methodologies proven to be ineffective.

> Unfortunately, we are coming to understand that the basic things we do in American schools—what we teach and how—*don't* work; we don't empower kids, don't nurture literacy, don't produce efficient workers, don't raise responsible citizens, don't create a functional democracy. If we really want to change student achievement in American schools, we must act directly on teaching and learning. More of the same is not the answer. (Zemelman, Daniels, and Hyde 1998)

Clearly the time has come for a new vision of what learning and education can be.

A Different Future for Theatre Education?

> It is the artist who must midwife the new reality that we . . . eagerly await.
> —Viola Spolin

Can this view of the current state of general education be a rallying call to theatre educators? I have seen theatre teachers who do empower students, nurture literacy, and teach responsible work ethics and characteristics of healthy citizenry. What is happening in these theatre classrooms that has eluded many other teachers? What makes some theatre programs grow and thrive while others die, stall, or are marginalized? Might theatre teachers bring another view of education to the table?

Dee Hock, in his forward-thinking work, *Birth of the Chaordic Age*, gives me reason for hope as I pursue answers to these questions.

In truth, there are no problems "out there." And there are no experts "out there" who could solve them if there were. The problem is "in here," in the depth of the collective consciousness of the species. When that consciousness begins to understand and grapple with the false Industrial Age concepts of organizations to which it clings; when it is willing to risk loosening the hold of those concepts and embrace new possibilities; when those possibilities engage enough minds, new patterns will emerge and we will find ourselves on the frontier of institutional alternatives ripe with hope and rich with possibilities. (Hock 1999, 78)

Theatre teachers who grapple with Industrial Age thinking and practices are pioneers on "the frontier of institutional alternatives ripe with hope and rich with possibilities" (78). If, as Hock asserts, the problems and solutions we are encountering at all levels of our society, including our schools, are not "out there" but "in here," we must confront in our own "consciousness" the threats to effective education in general and to effective theatre education in particular. It means changing the way we think about theatre education and letting that thinking shape our actions. It means looking anew at why we teach, whom we teach, what we teach, and how we teach.

Time is a significant factor. Most theatre teachers already feel overwhelmed with work responsibilities. Some see educational reform as change of such magnitude that most of us would not even have time to enter the conversation. And others may ask, "Can embracing change in this way really evolve more effective practice?"

As so many in this book testify, when even a few teachers reconsider their practice and make manageable changes in their classrooms or production work, it makes a difference—a difference in students' lives, the theatre program, and the school. Each step of change made by a teacher or teaching artist has an impact and is essential to the survival of theatre in our schools. I am convinced that this is practical and effective change we can hope for right now. Work at the national, state, and district levels can create a foundation and sow seeds for a shift in thought, but real change must be seen in what happens in a classroom each day between teacher and students. Without these changes, I question if theatre education will still be in the schools by the end of the twenty-first century.

Why Change Now?

Secondary school theatre education is at a crossroads in America. Down one road there are programs still in the box of Industrial Age thinking, removed from contemporary practice in theatre and emerging theories and methodologies in education. In these settings, theatre work with students is often hierarchical, teacher-centered, and is an attenuated or dated version of college or conservatory study. Focus in some schools is almost exclusively on the production of plays and musicals from the Broadway and regional theatre repertoire—more often than not unrelated to the lives of the majority of students in the school community. In many schools, theatre work is undervalued, fragmented, and accessible only after school and mostly to white, middle-class, able-bodied students (Lazarus 2000, 38). In a time of budget cuts coupled with the ever-shifting sea of education reforms, theatre education programs around the country are eroding. In many areas, as personnel move or retire and funding shifts to other priorities, theatre education is losing ground. Some states are not offering or are discontinuing certification of theatre teachers. Despite national and state standards in the arts, theatre as an academic subject is not mandated to be taught, and, in fact, is a classroom subject rarely offered in many states.

Zemelman, Daniels, and Hyde (1998) speak to these problems, which affect the presence and quality of arts education across the country.

> Lately, the role of the arts in public education has weakened even further. . . . Since 1990, forty-five states have slashed arts funding. . . . Arts teachers have been let go, programs dropped, and time allocations distorted, while class loads for the surviving arts specialists swell to ludicrous numbers. In its report *Creative America*, the President's Committee on the Arts and Humanities [1997, 17] bluntly describes the arts programming of the average American school as "impoverished or nonexistent." (13)

From this vantage point, I see a theatre education legacy of gross inequities in both access to and quality of programs, personnel, and facilities across communities and the nation (2000, 37). As more and more parents are those who have never taken a theatre class or attended a live theatre performance, we will likely see a drop in attendance and support for professional, community, and educational theatre across the population (37).

This is a pretty bleak view of the present state of theatre education in the United States, but it is a snapshot of a good deal of current practice in our schools and communities. If change is to occur, we, as pioneers, must have the courage to look unabashedly at all versions of *what is.*

Fortunately there are other views of *what is* theatre education. From the crossroads where we now stand, I see other directions in which the field is headed. This is the frontier of "alternatives ripe with hope and rich with possibilities," as Hock says (1999, 78). When I take in this view, I hear teachers and students speaking with a very different passion and vision. This practice involves the design and implementation of comprehensive, integrated curricula. It includes programs through which students are engaged in the exploration of social, historical, and educational issues through the study and production of theatre (38). This theatre education is learner-centered, socially responsible, provocative, and connected to the world in which students live. This is theatre education facilitated by teachers who understand the power of theatre to give voice to young people's concerns and ideas while connecting them to real and fictional figures throughout time. Embraced successfully by novice and veteran teachers, this approach is what I am calling best practice in theatre education.

Best Practice

Growing out of the frenzy surrounding the educational reform movements of the last two decades and grounded in a desire to effect lasting change in "actual, day-to-day teaching and learning" (Zemelman, Daniels, Hyde 1998, vii), the notion of best practice in education emerged. It was birthed by veteran teachers Steven Zemelman, Harvey Daniels, and Arthur Hyde. The term was borrowed from the legal and medical professions to describe "solid, reputable, state-of-the-art work in a field" (1998, viii). Zemelman and his colleagues describe a practitioner of best practice as

> someone who is following best practice standards, is aware of current research, and consistently offers clients the full benefits of the latest knowledge, technology, and procedures. . . . In education we generally haven't had such an everyday standard; on the contrary, some veteran teachers will even deny the significance of current research or new standards of instruction. . . . One wonders how long such self-satisfied teachers would continue to go to a doctor who says, "I practice medicine exactly the same way today that I did thirty years ago. I haven't changed a thing. I don't hold with all that newfangled stuff." (viii)

Zemelman's team was impelled by their experiences in the classroom and as specialists in curriculum and staff development. They drew from professional associations in each discipline and from research centers as they gathered "the current, national consensus recommendations about 'best educational practice'" in various curricular areas (vii). What they discovered was a high level of agreement across dissimilar fields about "how kids learn best." They culled their findings into thirteen "interlocking principles, assumptions, or theories" (7–8). Then, working with teachers in the Chicago public schools, they observed these principles in practice, documenting "teachers who were bringing them to life, practicing state-of-the-art instruction in their classrooms every day" (vii).

Zemelman, Daniels, and Hyde discovered that across most disciplines, authorities agreed about the principles of instruction that were best for student learning. Fundamentally, these principles were nothing new, just merely "misplaced" in the moves through Industrial Age and Technological Age thinking. While somewhat reminiscent of the progressive educational reform movements of the 1930s and 1960s, best practice principles of learning build on the strengths of that work and link it to current research about cognition for a lasting impact on learning. (See Figure 1–1.)

Best Practice in Theatre Education

Before I heard about Zemelman, Daniels, and Hyde's work, I was beginning to gather ideas about effective secondary school theatre education based on my

Figure 1–1 *Principles of Best Practice Learning*

STUDENT-CENTERED. The best starting point for schooling is young people's real interests; all across the curriculum, investigating students' own questions should always take precedence over studying arbitrarily and distantly selected "content."

EXPERIENTIAL. Active, hands-on, concrete experience is the most powerful and natural form of learning. Students should be immersed in the most direct possible experience of the content of every subject.

HOLISTIC. Children learn best when they encounter whole ideas, events, and materials in purposeful contexts, not by studying subparts isolated from actual use.

AUTHENTIC. Real, rich complex ideas and materials are at the heart of the curriculum. Lessons or textbooks that water-down, control, or oversimplify content ultimately disempower students.

EXPRESSIVE. To fully engage ideas, construct meaning, and remember information, students must regularly employ the whole range of communicative media—speech, writing, drawing, poetry, dance, drama, music, movement, and visual arts.

REFLECTIVE. Balancing the immersion in experience and expression must be opportunities for learners to reflect, debrief, and abstract from their experiences what they have felt and thought and learned.

SOCIAL. Learning is always socially constructed and often interactional; teachers need to create classroom interactions that "scaffold" learning.

COLLABORATIVE. Cooperative learning activities tap the social power of learning better than competitive and individualistic approaches.

DEMOCRATIC. The classroom is a model community; students learn what they live as citizens of the school.

COGNITIVE. The most powerful learning comes when children develop true understanding of concepts through higher-order thinking associated with various fields of inquiry and through self-monitoring of their thinking.

DEVELOPMENTAL. Children grow through a series of definable but not rigid stages, and schooling should fit its activities to the developmental level of students.

CONSTRUCTIVIST. Children do not just receive content; in a very real sense, they re-create and reinvent every cognitive system they encounter, including language, literacy, and mathematics.

CHALLENGING. Students learn best when faced with genuine challenges, choices, and responsibility in their own learning.

(Zemelman, Daniels, and Hyde 1998, 7–8)

experiences as a high school theatre teacher, theatre artist, professional development coordinator for theatre teachers, and university theatre teacher educator. My ideas evolved into the Characteristics of Best Practice in Theatre Education as I observed and interviewed teachers and artists around the country. (See Figure 1–2.)

Figure 1–2 *Characteristics of Best Practice in Theatre Learning*

> **Learner-Centered Classroom and Production Work**
>
> The students' place at the center of the learning process is acknowledged, valued, and nurtured. Learning together, students and teacher pose questions, investigate and consider ideas from multiple perspectives, and reflect on discoveries. Content is correlated with familiar ideas, lived experiences, and relevant social issues. There is shared decision making and individual and collective action. Dialogue, collaboration, risk-taking, and experimentation are hallmarks of this practice.
>
> **Socially Responsible Practice**
>
> Students learn in, through, and about theatre as members of society and citizens of the school and the world. Material studied and produced is relevant to students and their communities and is developmentally appropriate. Students and adults show respect for each other, the program, and the art form in all formal and informal communications and interactions. The program is physically, academically, and socially accessible to all students in the school regardless of age, race, gender, religion, socioeconomic status, sexual orientation, physical ability, or disability.
>
> **Comprehensive Theatre Education**
>
> Instruction is holistic, authentic, and allows students to learn and practice collaboratively in the roles of actor, director, playwright, designer, technician, critic, researcher, and audience. Curricular and cocurricular work intertwines production, history, criticism, and aesthetics. Integration of theatre study and practice takes place across arts disciplines, in other subjects, and in the school and community.

These three characteristics overlap and intersect in many ways within an effective theatre program. Based on recurring themes culled from the more than one hundred interviews and observations I conducted with teachers, artists, and others involved with theatre education, I also compiled common elements of effective practice. (See Figure 1–3.) Teacher-artists whose work is characterized in this way effectively and responsibly engage young people in learning. These characteristics and elements embody the principles of best practice in learning identified by Zemelman, Daniels, and Hyde, and they are central to an effective twenty-first century theatre education program.

These characteristics represent the qualities of teaching and learning that speak most to my heart and connect most with why I chose to become a theatre teacher in the first place. I am encouraged by the fact that they also speak to the heart of so many other theatre teachers and resonate with the work of Zemelman, his colleagues, and large numbers of teachers from other disciplines.

So What's New?

Reading Zemelman's list of the principles of best practice in learning, many of us will see we already draw on a number of the principles in our theatre classrooms every day. With, and often without, conscious planning, our students work

Figure 1–3 *Common Elements of Best Practice in Theatre Education*

- The teacher-artist's primary focus is on teaching *students* vs. teaching *theatre.* The study and practice of theatre is the means and method for effectively teaching students.
- The program encourages students to value theatre as an art form, profession, and lifelong interest.
- Students are actively engaged in high-quality theatre making in classroom work and productions.
- A process versus product construct is seen as a false dichotomy.
- Community and ensemble building is fundamental to the success of the program.
- The program encourages students to value themselves and others.
- Theatre classes and cocurricular productions are equally valued as learning opportunities.
- Productions are often viewed as laboratories for applying class instruction, and instruction and artmaking are imbedded in both classes and productions.
- There is a component of the program that focuses on creation of new works with, and, or by students.
- Theatre is seen as a catalyst for civic dialogue. Social issues are considered and explored through the art form in the classroom, production work, and activities in the school and community.
- The implicit political nature of theatre provides a forum for exploration, reflection, and expression of self and society.
- Theatre is seen as potentially about any topic and therefore is fertile ground for cross-curricular study.
- Classroom and production work is used to connect the past, present, and future to the lives of students and vice versa.
- The teacher asks for help and actively involves students, teachers, administrators, parents, and community members in appropriate roles in the program.
- Risk taking and change, while scary, is embraced.

In fewer cases, although not the exception, the following Common Elements were also present

- Outside funding through grants or artist-in-residence programs is actively pursued to enhance or extend the school program.
- Partnerships with and employment at local colleges, universities, and theatres is common and seen as of mutual benefit to the teacher and their partner organization or institution.
- Supportive administrators are seen as a critical factor to the program's success.
- The National Standards movement is seen as an important catalyst for precipitating change in theatre education at the local level.

collaboratively and experientially. Theatre education by its very nature can be student-centered, reflective, democratic, social, holistic, and developmentally appropriate. Auditions, productions, and classroom work can be as complex and authentic as in professional practice. Active learning, reflection, and cognitive experiences can be central to a theatre lesson or rehearsal. *Can* be. Countless articles, research projects, and conference sessions have indeed promoted theatre education as a sort of cure-all for what ails our students and schools today. The *potential* of theatre education as best practice seems boundless.

But the operative word in best practice is *practice*. It implies action. Until I *act* on my knowledge of best practice, unless I *practice* these principles in deliberate ways day to day, the potential of theatre education is just an unfulfilled promise. *Nothing changes*. It's like learning that there is a marvelous gift for me in a place just beyond my vantage point, but then not taking the time—or being too afraid, complacent, or arrogant—to move so I can see it, receive it, and use it.

No one claims perfect adherence to this level of practice, however, and it can be scary to work in a new way or from an unfamiliar perspective. We are each on an individual journey toward best practice. It is a direction toward which we are moving. No one is starting at the same point or having to travel the same distance with the same students or across the same terrain. The journeys taken by each teacher-artist in this book represent a broad range of professional and educational experiences, student populations served, budgets, facilities, and also the size, condition, and support for their programs. These and other factors influence their day-to-day work with students. Their practice is grounded in a willingness to be pioneers, to make change, to grow their practice as artists and teachers. They each, in their own way, embody the spirit, if not the full letter, of best practice in theatre education.

On the Verge: The Pioneer's Journey

In his play *On the Verge (or The Geography of Yearning)* Eric Overmyer depicts the trek of three so-called lady adventurers as they travel through Terra Incognita from the end of the nineteenth century forward into the future of the late twentieth century (Overmeyer 1993). In the closing pages of the play, two of the travelers elect to remain in the comfort of the mid-twentieth century. They ask the third what she envisions of her trek forward. Mary, the third traveler, "osmoses" into a trancelike state in which she sees a vision of the future whose meaning she doesn't fully understand.

Somewhat like Mary, I feel I have just glimpsed the possibilities of a theatre education that respects students as colearners and collaborators, one that engages a wide cross section of students in respectful practice and study of the art form. This is theatre education that is relevant, integrated, challenging, and comprehensive. It is not a destination but a journey through the Terra Incognita of secondary school theatre where young people are engaged in active learning, inquiry, and artmaking and where the potential of theatre can be realized. But this is a journey for which there aren't tried-and-true waymarks, maps, and well-traveled highways. You can see just the merest glimmers of this practice as you embark. But remember, it is a journey that is self-defined and charted by reshaping, recycling, and reinventing theatre education anew in your classroom and school. And there are sturdy pioneers on the path with you (Lazarus 2000).

Overmyer closes his play with Mary's words as she glimpses the journey awaiting her. "Billions of new worlds, waiting to be discovered. Explored and illuminated. . . . I am on the verge" (Overmeyer 1993). The remainder of this book is for those who are also "on the verge." It is my hope that reading and referencing this book will encourage a shift in thinking, an embracing of new possibilities, and a practice that can effect lasting change. This is a call to all of us to shift our vision of what secondary school theatre education can be. It is a call to make it so. I believe it's why we went into this field in the first place.

Ideas for Further Reflection

Questions to Consider

- What in my world has changed in the last year? What has stayed the same?
- How has change and stasis affected my life? My school? My program?
- Which of my students has been affected by change and how?
- How does my program reflect a response to change?
- Who might be traveling or willing to travel on this journey toward best practice with me? Who are the advocates for change and the mentors in my school? Are there others in my life outside of school who can serve as a support network, a community of change-seekers and change-makers?

What's On Your Mind?

Reflective practice—the habit of considering and reconsidering what transpires in your interactions with students and others—is an important element of best practice. As busy professionals, we often don't take time for reflection or dismiss it as reminiscent of homework assignments. But there are all kinds of wondering and worries swirling about us each day that beg reflection. As you consider the ideas in this chapter in relation to your practice, what anecdotes or incidents come to mind? Begin a journal in which you freewrite about what you are thinking related to events that happen or have happened in your work. End each entry with "It Made Me Think. . . ." Don't include what it made you think *about*; just describe the incident and that you are thinking about it. Like Professor Dumbledore's pensive in *Harry Potter and the Goblet of Fire* (Rowling 2000), this metacognition allows you to take your thoughts out and look at them over time. You might find patterns or recurring themes to help you in your journey toward best practice.

Mapping Your Journey

When facing change, it is helpful to think from a new perspective or find a new medium of expression. To this end, take out a sheet of paper and a pen, pencil, or marker. Freedraw a "map" of your journey to this point in your career. Draw straight, curved, zigzag, or a combination of lines that capture the path you have traveled thus far as a theatre teacher-artist. Identify by symbols or words the events, people, interactions, and opportunities that were high points, low points, obstacles, and incentives along the way. When did you feel you were moving in a direction you wanted to head? When were you lost or wandering? Discuss your map with a trusted colleague, family member, or friend, or do some freewriting about patterns you notice, things to celebrate, and thoughts that emerged as you drew. What did you learn about where you've been in your journey that can help in your next steps?

> Not all who wander are lost.
> —J. R. R. Tolkien

Where Do You Want to Go? Appreciative Inquiry[2] and Best Practice

Whether you are a preservice theatre teacher or a veteran of many years, cultivation of a vision of where you can go in your practice is liberating and allows for change that often doesn't seem possible.

WHAT IS?

Draft a shorthand description of *what is*—a brief account of the best in your present practice and/or program. Look over the characteristics of best practice in theatre education and the common elements of best practice (Figures 1–2 and 1–3 on pages 9 and 10) and quickly list ways in which you actively engage in best practice now.

WHAT COULD BE?

Now for a fun part. Get a new piece of paper.

- What are some of the heartfelt hopes stirring in you about theatre education and your practice? Jot down your thoughts.

- What is one powerful moment or experience that stands out as a time when you felt particularly effective, challenged, alive as a teacher? When did you feel you were using your full capacities and were able to draw out the most positive and the best in the students you were working with? Add this information to your notes.

- If people who know the very best about you were asked to name the three best qualities or capabilities you bring to teaching, what would they say? Add this to your notes.

- Who has stood out in your life as an example of a great teacher? What was or is it like to be around this person? How has this person inspired you? How did this person work and live? Write these down. (Note that often the qualities we admire in others are the qualities we too possess!)

WHAT OUGHT TO BE?

Imagine for a minute that you have fallen sound asleep. You awaken five years later. While you were sleeping, many changes happened, small and large. Theatre education, and your work in particular, was reconstituted in ways you would most like to see for yourself, your students, your school, your community, and the field. You wake up and go into the world to take a full view of these changes. You are happy with what you see. It's a view of the kind of work you most want to be part of.

- What are some highlights you see? What is happening that is new, better, healthy, and good? Write these on a new list.
- If you had been awake during this time, how might *you* have brought about these changes? Add to the list of notes.
- Visualize the projects, practices, and partnerships that were developed, created and used. What do they look like? Jot these down.

> We must form perfect models in thought and look at them continually, or we shall never carve them out in grand and noble lives.
> *—Mary Baker Eddy*

Figure 1–4 *Journey On!*

Now, if anything is possible, how would you ignite or be an agent for positive change in your work? Add these thoughts to your notes. Save these ideas. Expand and revise them as you read this book. Continue to envision more and more as you take each step on your journey.

Selected Resources

In addition to the works cited in this chapter, the following serve as sources of interesting ideas for further reflection.

Arts Education Partnership. 2002. *Critical Links: Learning in the Arts and Student Academic and Social Development.* Washington, DC: Arts Education Partnership.

Sergiovanni, Thomas. J. 1992. *Moral Leadership: Getting to the Heart of School Improvement.* San Francisco: Jossey-Bass.

Zander, Rosamund Stone, and Benjamin Zander. 2000. *The Art of Possibility.* Boston: Harvard Business School Press.

Notes

1. David O'Fallon was Director of Education at the National Endowment for the Arts. He later became Executive Director of the Perpich Center for Arts Education, a state agency in Minnesota that houses a high school of the arts, a research center, and a professional development institute. David is now president of the McPhail Center for the Arts, a community-based arts organization in Minneapolis (O'Fallon 2002).

2. Appreciative Inquiry (AI) was developed by David Cooperrider, a specialist in organizational development at Case Western Reserve University. AI contrasts with other problem-solving methods which present organizations, large or small, as "problems-to-be-solved." Instead, AI invites change by looking at the best of *what is*, the best of *what should be*, and ultimately *what will be.* This is a view of an organization as a solution-to-be-embraced (Cooperrider and Whitney 1999; Cooperrider, Sorensen, Whitney, and Yeager 2000).

WHOSE PROGRAM IS THIS?

Questions on the Journey Toward Best Practices
An Introduction to Chapters 2, 3, and 4

What we're about is unity, diversity, talent, [and] respect. Those are kind of the key words for us. . . . I work with racially diverse kids. . . . A lot of [students] are not used to revealing themselves to people of other races, backgrounds, sexual preferences. They come in with all kinds of barriers in terms of what adults are about in their lives. . . . The very first thing I say to the kids is that it's my challenge to get you to trust, and I'm for real. . . . I tell them how I came to this work and why it's important to me and then we go into a variety of theatre exercises that develop safe space for an individual and for a group. Safe space is also something that you have to continually work on; it doesn't just appear and then it's there. You tell certain things to your family or to your folk that you don't reveal to other people. [This] . . . also makes for a really volatile classroom because as soon as everybody knows everything about you, if any violation happens, it's much bigger than just an argument in any kind of class. . . . By knowing your kids, you really get a sense of. . . . what to do.

—Jan Mandell, Teacher

- Who is a secondary school theatre program for?
- Who is served in the program and how?
- Who isn't served and why?
- How are students' lived experiences part of their study and practice of theatre?
- What is socially responsible and socially engaged theatre education?
- How can a theatre program serve as a catalyst for dialogue and exploration of self and society?
- What is an effective balance between instruction, reflection, aesthetics, history, criticism, and production?

- What is the relationship between the theatre curriculum and other academic subjects offered in the school?
- What do the qualities of best practice in theatre education look like in the classroom and rehearsal space?

In the next three chapters, teachers and artists reflect on these and other questions. In Chapter 2, theatre teacher-artists share learner-centered practices for classroom and production settings, and in Chapter 3 multiple ways in which they create socially engaged and socially responsible programs are discussed. Chapter 4 considers comprehensive and integrated approaches to theatre education. Characteristics of best practice in theatre education is discussed throughout with the full understanding that the characteristics are not mutually exclusive. In the classroom or in rehearsals, they overlap, merge, emerge, and blend. In the best of all situations, and for a few teachers, all of the characteristics are fully present in their programs.

Changes in practice evolve differently for each teacher and unfold over an entire career. A teacher with gifts in learner-centered practice may not yet use discipline-based methodologies or explore curriculum in an integrated or socially engaged manner. Directors who stage socially responsible plays tied to the school curriculum may still direct in a traditional, director-centered style. Change is a journey we take as individuals and the rate and shape of our journey will be unique to our individual circumstances. It is the movement on the journey, toward or away from best practice, which should be considered. This book shares multiple views of this journey.

Clarifying Terms

It might be helpful here to clarify some terms I am using in the discussion of production work in secondary schools. I use the term *learner-centered* versus *performer-centered* because I want to highlight practices appropriate to those still learning about theatre. I also want to acknowledge that everyone involved in producing theatre—performer and nonperformer—is essential to the production. I wish to highlight best practice in devising and production work with performers *and* student directors, designers, dramaturgs, playwrights, crew members, and stage managers and to align production activity with artmaking, classroom work, and lifelong learning. I also want to disrupt the hierarchy that can dog a program when those onstage are given more prominent and powerful positions in a theatre program than "the techies" and those who are literally behind the scenes. To this end, I also use the word *company* to refer to all engaged in work on a given production. I use specific terminology where appropriate, for clarity, or emphasis.

I use the term *theatre* to refer to any performative event with students. Theatre, as an art form, continues to evolve. The lines between theatre, dance, music, art, and film are blending and blurring. Using *theatre* is more efficient in this context

A student-actor must learn that "how to act" . . . is inextricably bound up with every other person in the complexity of the art form.

—*Viola Spolin*

than calling up *plays*, *musicals*, *movement pieces*, *performance*, *site specific*, *interactive*, or *improvisational work* each time I refer to performance with students. I use the words *play* or *production* for similar reasons. I mean to refer to whatever performance piece students are producing.

I continue to employ the terms *teacher*, *artist*, and *director* interchangeably or use them in combination, as in *teacher-director* or *teacher-artist* to emphasize the multiple roles these professionals assume when working with students and young artists.

2 *Learner-Centered Practice*

The teacher cannot be the only expert in the classroom. To deny students their own expert knowledge is to disempower them.

—LISA DELPIT

Theatre is a language through which human beings can engage in active dialogue on what is important to them. It allows individuals to create a safe space that they may inhabit in groups and use to explore the interactions which make up their lives. It is a lab for problem solving, for seeking options, and for practicing solutions.

—AUGUSTO BOAL

What Is Learner-Centered Practice?

What is the nature of learner-centered practice? What does it look like in theatre classroom and production settings? Margaret Wheatley (1994),[1] a specialist in organizational communication, has thought a lot about ownership and the role it plays in a meaningful connection to groups and organizations. Her ideas have special relevance to our students' investment in their own education.

> At first [the students] thought I . . . didn't know the answers because I would ask them questions . . . trying to get them to disover the answer. . . . It's a whole concept of ownership.
>
> —Kent Sorensen, Teacher

> Ownership describes the personal links to the organization [school, class, program], the charged, emotion-driven *feeling* that can inspire people. . . . We know that the best way to build ownership is to give over the creation process to those who will be charged with its implementation. We are never successful if we merely present a plan in finished form to employees [students]. It doesn't work to just ask people to sign on when they haven't been involved in the design process, when they haven't experienced the plan as a living, breathing thing. (Wheatley 1994, 66)

Can we "give over" our theatre classrooms to students and allow access so they "sign on" without chaos ensuing? How do we fairly accommodate everyone's voice and incorporate everyone's ideas? What about teacher accountability and classroom management? The answers to these questions are at the core of learner-centered practice.

19

Learner-Centered Practice in the Classroom

> The child shall have the right to freedom of expression: this right shall include freedom to seek, receive and impart information and ideas of all kinds . . . either orally, in writing or in print, in the form of art, or through any other media of the child's choice.
>
> —UN Convention on the Rights of the Child, Article 13

Learner-centered teaching is not a student-led or child-driven approach to teaching in which the learners make all decisions regardless of their emotional, social, or academic maturity. In learner-centered instruction, teachers assesses the skills and interests of students and then structure meaningful learning experiences that engage everyone in a democratic classroom environment. Learning together, students and teachers pose questions, consider ideas from multiple perspectives, investigate topics, and reflect on discoveries.

Learner-centered practice is the opposite of what Freire (1996) refers to as "the banking concept of education." In this approach, "the scope of action allowed to students extends only as far as receiving, filing, and storing the deposits." Freire contrasts this with an education that liberates, claiming "[e]ducation must begin with the solution of the teacher-student contradiction . . . so that both are simultaneously teachers *and* students" (53). Discussing learning that is student-

Figure 2–1 *A student-designed poster for a high school production of* The Diary of Anne Frank

centered, Zemelman, Daniels, and Hyde (1998) state "The best starting point for school is young people's real interests; all across the curriculum, investigating students' own questions should always take precedence over studying arbitrarily and distantly selected 'content'" (8).

In learner-centered practice, both teachers and students raise questions and shape learning opportunities. All discover answers while learning information and skills in the curriculum. For example, while reading *The Diary of Anne Frank*[2] in an Introduction to Theatre class, students may question the interpretation of a particular role, depiction of setting, or the various political and social issues in the play. Students also may be concerned about a war in their own country. The teacher might encourage them to shape their concerns about war into questions. Students can then investigate how theatre artists and others have explored similar questions or have faced and endured war. Students can then develop and share various design, dramaturgical, playwriting, or performance projects that further investigate their questions. Learning then can be related back to the play and the students' lives. Additional questions may be framed for further study during the semester.

Middle school teacher Deb Alexander did just this. She designed a theatre curriculum using *The Diary of Anne Frank* as a springboard into the exploration of themes and topics of interest to her students. This curriculum is described in Chapter 4 on pages 114–132.

Teacher-Student Relationships in a Learner-Centered Program

"Who is in charge?" In a learner-centered program, the role of the teacher, not as peer or friend, but as the responsible adult in the classroom, is understood by all. The teacher appropriately shares authority by creating an atmosphere of mutual trust, openness, risk-taking, and problem solving. Adjustments in instruction and changes in direction or methodology prompted by the teacher and/or the students deepen and enhance everyone's learning and participation. Dialogue—an ongoing exchange of ideas and opinions—is fundamental, as is assessment of the students' academic, artistic, social, developmental, and emotional needs. With this information, teachers evaluate each student's ability to make and act on decisions of all kinds.

Decision-making flexibility is key in a learner-centered program. Variations in instructional methods and projects occur since many students are self-directed and self-motivated. Some work independently while others learn best in pairs or groups. Projects that accommodate a range of learning styles and decision-making abilities are also built into each unit. Instruction and assignments within a given unit may vary from student to student and class to class as content is related to familiar ideas, lived experiences, and relevant social issues. Discussion about who is making which decisions, why, and how is part of everyone's reflective practice, creating a dynamic classroom environment monitored by the teacher, but shaped by everyone involved in the learning community.

Figure 2–2 *Teachers and students in learner-centered classrooms are engaged in reflective practice.*

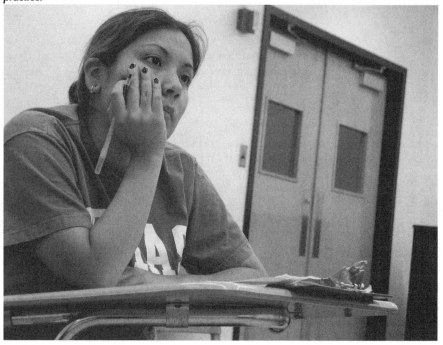

Participation in a Learner-Centered Program

[Participation is] the fundamental right of citizenship . . . the process of sharing decisions which affect one's life and the life of the community in which one lives.

—ROGER HART

Involvement in real-life experiences and projects in which students have ownership and investment is authentic participation. For example, a group of students elect to be dramaturgs for the upcoming play their school is producing. They research and prepare background material to help the actors better understand the play. They write program notes and install a display of their research adjacent to the theatre. They are engaged in projects akin to those of professional dramaturgs. They are also self-directed and invested because they have ownership of all phases of the project. They are participating in an authentic manner, as opposed to students who simply write a research paper for their teacher about the play.

Sue Scarborough talks about how she includes authentic participation and decision making in her classroom.

[Learner-centered work] is in every lesson. After a monologue or scene I ask them "how did it go for you?" I start with them. . . . Empowerment of the students is a big thing with me. . . I start very simply by not having them raise their hands. If they have something to say they can say it as long as no one else is talking. . . . It seems so simple to adults. We don't raise our hands when we have something to say. In education the teacher has the power to decide who can talk and when. . . . By giving [students] back this power . . . they talk and listen . . . to each other. (2003)

Roger Hart (deWinter 1997) adopted a "ladder of participation," showing a progression from synthetic to authentic participation, to characterize children's decision-making involvement in various worldwide projects. (See Figure 2–3.) Of the eight rungs on this ladder, however, only the top three are truly learner-centered.

For years I assumed my students were participating in authentic ways because I assigned them responsibilities and informed them or consulted them about various projects. The most dynamic theatre education programs, however, regularly embody shared decision-making and student-initiated or student-directed experiences like those on the upper rungs of Harts' model. In true learner-centered programs, students have a palpable "ownership," as Wheatley describes it (1994, 66).

> Sometimes . . . [I try] to shape things and the child will say "This doesn't make any sense, Miss Clunie. . . We should do it this way."
> —Gloria Bond Clunie, Teacher and Playwright

Drama in a Learner-Centered Program

I was . . . hesitant to work with middle-school kids and have them create their own drama. I thought it would be very hokey and wouldn't have much depth. . . . I got the kids working . . . and the classes came up with important issues that they were dealing with . . . [like] the topic of judging others. . . . After about a week . . . we had the Columbine tragedy here. . . . The kids were being bombarded with the media. I had the counselors come in. . . . We talked about what could [drive] a kid . . . to the point that he would do something like that. . . . The students decided they wanted to do [their devised piece] in the hallway . . . because that's where most of this stuff—all the judgment—happens. . . . [We had] the audience sit in the middle and the action . . . [happened] around the audience. These kids [created] something [through drama] that [was] important and that could make a difference in somebody's life.

—Brianna Lindahl, Teacher

What learner-centered teaching and directing strategies are useful for theatre teachers to know? Laura McCammon (2002a) emphasizes that when young people assume significant responsibilities and form healthy relationships with adults and each other they are able to move successfully through adolescence into adulthood. She believes that this is "particularly true in process or role drama structures or those employing Heathcote's Mantle of the Expert" (Heathcote and Bolton 1995). As Laura points out, this informal drama work, also labeled *creative drama*, *role drama*, *applied drama*, or *process drama*, is frequently overlooked at the secondary level as a dynamic learner-centered tool (McCammon 2002a, 9). A number of secondary school theatre teachers I spoke with however, regularly draw from drama practitioners like Heathcote, Boal, O'Neill, Neelands, Grady,

Figure 2–3 *Ladder of Participation*

LEVEL 8: YOUTH-INITIATED, SHARED DECISIONS WITH ADULTS: Hart sees influence shared between children and adults as the final goal of participation. He cites a project in a New York City high school in which students, concerned about the increasing dropout rate due to teen pregnancy, organized a coalition for better sex education in the school.

LEVEL 7: YOUTH-INITIATED AND DIRECTED: Youth conceive, organize, and direct a project themselves, without adult interference. Except in natural play, examples of this level of participation are hard to find, says Hart, because adults have difficulty honoring children's initiatives and leaving them to manage those initiatives themselves.

LEVEL 6: ADULT-INITIATED, SHARED DECISIONS WITH YOUTH: Hart sees this level of participation mostly in the case of projects concerned with community development in which initiators, such as policy makers, community workers, and local residents, involve a variety of age ranges and interest groups. One project he cites is the "Nuestro Parque" project in East Harlem. Teens, young children, and parents designed a neighborhood park and involved their community in the development and review of model plans.

LEVEL 5: CONSULTED AND INFORMED: Youth are consulted extensively about a project designed and operated by adults. An example of this kind of participation is a New York television station, which regularly consults and pilots their programming to a panel of children.

LEVEL 4: ASSIGNED BUT INFORMED: Adults call in youth to participate and inform them how and why they are to be involved. Only after the young people understand the intentions of the project and the purpose of their involvement do they decide whether to take part. Hart provides the example of the children who served as pages during the World Summit for Children. They were called in as a visible presence toward compelling the leaders attending to make significant changes.

LEVEL 3: TOKENISM: Youth are apparently given a voice, but this is to serve the child-friendly image adults want to create rather than the interest of the youth themselves. According to Hart, this is common practice in the Western world, for instance, on conference panels, where the radiating charm of children often makes a great impression.

LEVEL 2: DECORATION: Youth are called to embellish adult actions, for instance, by song, dance, and other affecting activities. Adults do not, however, pretend that all this is in the interest of the children themselves.

LEVEL 1: MANIPULATION: Youth are engaged or used for their own benefit as determined by adults, while the youth themselves do not understand the implications of their involvement. For example, toddlers carrying banners in a demonstration for family rights.

Adapted with permission (De Winter 1997)

Tarlington, and Rohd. Teacher-directors find interactive informal drama techniques engaging for students because they provide structures through which students can think critically, ask questions, frame points of view, make decisions, take action, and face the consequences of their actions.

A study conducted in an urban middle school with students infamous for chronic discipline problems illustrates the impact informal drama can have on secondary school students (Nelson, Colby, and McIlrath 2001). The middle-school students in the study participated in a series of five drama sessions. They took on the roles of faculty members in an alternative school, college students, grand jurors, family therapists, social workers, and army personnel. They explored issues of discrimination, segregation, and inequity. A drama specialist actively drew on students' lived experiences as they interacted with their teacher in and out of role. In each session, students had decision-making authority, control, and power, and their voices were actively sought out and heard.

> What was unmistakable, not only to the researchers but to the administration and to the teachers in the school, was a sudden and dramatic shift in the learning behavior of this particularly challenged group of students. The cause of this change in the behavioral and social dynamics clearly lay in the power of role to free each individual's voice and allow its expression, to provide a context that empowers students to make decisions, control outcomes and observe the consequences of their ideas in action. Finally, drama legitimatizes held knowledge and allows students to build new learning on old. (67)

When we use drama like this across the curriculum and for exploration of issues of interest to learners in our classrooms and productions, we have a powerful tool to liberate young people as artists and human beings. The learner-centered dramas like those previously described and in the lesson and rehearsal ideas shared at the end of this chapter are but a few examples of this dynamic approach to best practice.

Rebecca Jallings (2002) teaches high-school theatre at West High School in Madison, Wisconsin. She describes how her students helped her rethink and develop a learner-centered practice.

> I started teaching at West as a forty-year-old woman who had lived my life in a pretty white world. . . . I had . . . black kids in my Theatre I classes [and]. . . . I just couldn't stand the way I was with them. . . . I was always sure I was going to say the wrong thing or do the wrong thing. So . . . I went out and tried to find books on how to make this sort of translation for myself. . . . Of course, they don't exist, or they didn't then.
>
> Then . . . the [Madison] Rep did *Fires in the Mirror* by Anna Deveare Smith. . . . I hired . . . a Black actor from Chicago . . . [to come] into my class. . . . He worked with the kids in theatre and talked about issues of race. . . . At the same exact time I was starting to work on my Master's degree. . . . I was videotaping small groups as they worked on their movement projects. . . . I would just turn the camera on and let it run.
>
> So, I'm being bombarded with all these ideas [from the guest actor] and . . . I'm looking at the tapes of the kids in my classes. . . . [In] every single one . . . the black kid is in the circle but one step physically backed out of the circle, or half turned away from the circle. And the black kids are completely quiet. They don't say anything. They do what they're told by the white kids . . . they just don't offer any ideas. And they're just barely . . . connected.
>
> I'm thinking to myself, "I have created [a safe] environment in a theatre class . . . but . . . I have completely silenced the black kids cause they have bought into the idea that we're all going to be nicer to each other here than we are in the rest of the school." . . . It was as if they'd been co-opted into shutting up. . . . The black kids didn't want to be unfriendly. They weren't going to be disruptive because they liked me, they liked the class. . . . But it certainly wasn't their stuff that they were doing; it was the white kids' stuff.

Rebecca decided to interview her students about their project.

Some of the white kids were really damning of the black kids: "They didn't do anything. They just sort of stood around. We had to always call her back to work." I was just horrified. . . . [The black kids] . . . said that the project really didn't have anything to do with them and that the music they used . . . didn't relate to them in any way and . . . "Why were [the white girls] rude?" . . . I said . . . "Did you act on that at all? Did you say anything to them?" . . . [They said] "No, we didn't want to . . . do that." . . . [One student] said "I get along with white kids OK. White kids got more money than I do. They have better lives than I do, but I get along with them. We all have the same class." . . . This was his reason for keeping quiet during class. I was . . . heartbroken.

I got my student teacher to make transcripts of the tapes [from the kids interviews] . . . and I made a play out of it like *Fires in the Mirror*. I took exactly what the kids said in these small group projects . . . and I wrote it into a play. At the end of the semester . . . they wanted to see it. . . . I said . . . "How about if the kids who are in it view it first and if they're comfortable with it, then yes, we'll read it in class." Not only did they say "OK," but they all read their own parts.

I'm really comfortable talking to my kids now. . . . I realized that I get to make mistakes. And then you say you're sorry. You say "Explain it to me, and I'll understand." . . . You finally figure out that [as in] everything else in life, the only way you're going to get anywhere is by trying it and being ready to say you're sorry. . . . Now . . . if there's something I don't understand about what they're saying, what they're doing, I don't brush it off. I stop and say "Wait a minute, what does that mean? Explain that to me. I'm very white. I'm fifty-four, explain that to me." Asking questions is an awful lot easier. (Jallings 2002)

Learner-Centered Practice in Productions: Balancing Art and Education

My intent with actors is to "feed them" in such a way that they arrive at the conclusion of the performance that they ultimately feel is theirs because they discovered it. What does it matter which of us put in whatever elements?

—Lloyd Richards, Director

I call it directing by intimidation. The director arrived just before the rehearsal for the musical began. He started barking at the cast and crew to get started. There were no explanations or greetings. Most of the kids onstage looked anxious, unsure, or confused about what was expected of them and why they were being yelled at. They did their best to please and appease him so he wouldn't throw one of his legendary tantrums and then storm out of rehearsal. "OK, now stand over there. That's right," he shouted. "No, turn toward the audience and hold your chest up. No, don't look at the floor. Look up. This is happy!" Later that week, a few students were in my room complaining to each other about this director. I wondered aloud why they kept auditioning for his shows if they were so dissatisfied with the experience. They looked at me blankly. "Because we want to be in the musical." It made me think.

"What should I do?" Kent asked. He was working on a scene from the show. He was shifting back and forth on his feet and his arms, dangling at his sides, seemed heavy and awkward. Kent meant, "What should I do with my body? Should I move? Look somewhere? Stand?" I said, "Well, Jeff" (his character's name), "where are you at this moment?" "In my room." "What are you doing when this scene begins?" "Avoiding my parents." "OK, here are some props you can work with if you'd like. Use whatever you need. This is your room. What might you be doing right now, at this specific moment, to avoid your parents?" The rehearsal progressed with me just asking questions, sidecoaching, and encouraging him and his scene partner to try lots of different choices. They explored and improvised action and dialogue related to the scene and then worked from the script. By the end of that rehearsal, they had found staging, business, line readings, and powerful moments of action and interaction that were comfortable for them and compelling for an audience. I didn't tell them what to do, when to do it, or how to do it, like I used to do. I didn't say "I want you to . . . " I just prompted them to consider the dramatic truth of each moment of the scene. I helped them generate choices for those moments and then we shaped those choices into playable action. They made the choices. They felt like actors. This is a whole new way of directing for me, but, with practice, I have come to love creating theatre in this way, with students.

Producing theatre for an audience is a gratifying and an essential culmination of theatre study for many young people. Productions can be especially meaningful when the experience is used as a laboratory for application of classroom instruction, investigation of dramatic or musical theatre literature, refinement of students' original work, and as a forum where students' interests and concerns can be voiced. Like learner-centered classroom work, learner-centered production work engages student performers, playwrights, directors, designers, technicians and dramaturgs in dialogue, decision making, and individual and collective action. The students' place at the center of the production process is acknowledged, valued, and nurtured. Collaboration, co-ownership, risk-taking, and experimentation are hallmarks of best practice theatre making with middle and high school students just as they have been in the professional practice of directors such as Anne Bogart, Lloyd Richards, Marshall Mason, Mark Lamos, Zelda Fischlander, and Gordon Davidson (Bartow 1988).

Learner-centered production work is dynamic and requires ongoing assessment of students' abilities, interests, and investment. Directing strategies grow from these assessments, ongoing dialogue with students, and directors' clear sense of their program's purpose and direction. These directors exhibit spontaneity and a willingness to be engaged in the creative process *with* young people. As Anne Bogart said, "directing is about feeling, about being in the room with other people—with actors, with designers, with an audience . . . about breathing and responding fully to the situation at hand, being able to plunge and encourage a plunge into the unknown at the right moment" (Dixon and Smith 1995, 9).

When some of the students in my Directing the Young Performer class at The University of Texas at Austin first experience my learner-centered directing style, they are skeptical about "plunging." Despite all they might have heard about professional directors who work collaboratively, some are doubtful that working this way with secondary school students can be successful. Most of them have worked with high school directors who started the rehearsal process with a read-through and table work without any script exploration or ensemble building. They then were launched into blocking sessions in which their directors told them where to move, how, and when. Now they are at the university and I am suddenly disrupting their conception of acting and directing. Some of them feel baffled or off-balance by work that invites the company into the theatre-making process and asks students for their opinions. Others feel this inclusionary way of working is a big waste of time or an unnecessary diversion. A student once commented, "When I was in high school no one ever asked us what we thought. We aren't used to that." Fortunately, after most of these students devise, adapt, and practice learner-centered strategies in their own directing projects, their views change. After using learner-centered approaches with her own high-school students, this same student enthusiastically commented, "It's the only way I direct now!"

> When a theater technique or stage convention is regarded as a ritual and the reason for its inclusion in the list of actors' skills is lost, it is useless. . . . No one separates batting a ball from the game itself.
>
> —VIOLA SPOLIN

Valerie Roberts Labonski (2002) teaches at Morton West High School in Berlin, Illinois. She describes a performance of Michael Frayn's uproarious play within a play, *Noises Off*. This experience shows the power of student ownership in a theatre program.

It's the end of the third act. Planned chaos is ensuing onstage. As Gary falls down the stairs he [unintentionally] clips the grocery box [with] the glass bottle of cider. The cider not only rolls down the stairs but off the stage into the house [and] the bottle shatters. So [the actors onstage] have their moment of discovery with Gary at the bottom of the stairs. Then Poppy, the assistant stage manager [in the world of the play] trots out—in character—with a broom and a dustpan. She quickly sweeps up the mess and trots off. As she is doing this [they] all . . . stop . . . and, in unison and in character, react to Poppy's clean up. A few seconds later Poppy comes back out with a mop. And they react again. It was hilarious.

After the show I went backstage with a neutral look on my face and asked Maria, the [actual] stage manager, whose idea it was to send out Poppy. She . . . said "It was mine." . . . I told her it was a brilliant idea. Then I asked how she came to that decision. [She said she had] talked it over with [the] student tech director and [the actor playing] Poppy. At first Maria was going to clean it up, but that would break the world of the play. Then they decided that Poppy wouldn't break [that] world . . . and when it was received so well, the mop seemed like the next logical thing to do. Then I talked to the actors, who, [as if] on cue, responded "acting is reacting," which I had been saying . . . throughout the rehearsal process. [Their] moment of discussion and decision making never would have happened if I had been backstage. They would have turned to me and [their] idea never would have crossed my mind. (Labonski 2002)

Key Questions

When teacher-directors discuss directing in learner-centered productions, they talk passionately and with enthusiasm about their artistry. They often discuss aesthetics, the quality of the dramatic material they produce, and their innovative and provocative use of production values. In addition, they speak about various educational, artistic, and ethical questions related to theatre making at the secondary level.

- Is directing young performers different than or the same as, directing adult actors?
- What is the ebb and flow between process and product?
- What are appropriate artistic standards for work with young artists?
- What are the intersections between classroom work and production work?
- What are the unique demands of learner-centered production work on student playwrights, directors, designers, and performers?
- How does a learner-centered program save time in the long run?

These questions are explored in the remainder of this chapter.

Directing Young Performers and Adult Performers

Michael Bloom, in his book *Thinking Like a Director*, reminds readers that one of the director's responsibilities is to determine "the story," how the playwright's ideas are interpreted and presented to an audience. He says, "One of the most important functions a director fulfills is determining, with the actors, and designers, which story to tell and how to tell it coherently" (Bloom 2001, 5). A director must engage the company in the storytelling process so that ideas are translated into images that make meaning for an audience.

When working with experienced actors, a director can assume the performers have skills, experience, and a certain degree of training with which to "tell the story." Seasoned, adult actors have a working knowledge not only of the art form of theatre but also of how to work in this art form. They understand fundamental rehearsal practices, terminology, methods, and procedures. Veteran actors know how to analyze a text, develop a character, take direction, and fully participate in the collaborative process.

With inexperienced performers, "telling the story" requires acquisition of the most basic information and skills. Most learner-centered teacher-directors feel young people do not effectively learn skills by rote or by replicating college or conservatory theatre programs that prescribe certain techniques. Spolin (1983) captures the problems with that approach.

Techniques are not mechanical devises—a neat little bag of tricks, each neatly labeled, to be pulled out by the actor when necessary. When the form of an art becomes static, these isolated "techniques" presumed to make the form are taught and adhered to strictly. Growth of both individual and form suffer thereby, for unless the student is unusually intuitive, such rigidity in teaching, because it neglects inner development, is invariably reflected in his performance.

When the actor knows "in his bones" there are many ways to do and say one thing, techniques will come (as they must) from his total self. For it is by direct, dynamic awareness of an acting experience that experience and techniques are spontaneously wedded, freeing the student for the flowing, endless pattern of stage behavior. (14)

This sense of student actors-as-learners is central to best practice. Teachers in a learner-centered program teach strategies to help young performers grow in their understanding and practice of the theatre. These strategies—bridges necessary to build between young people and the artform—are less necessary when working with seasoned performers.

Process-Centered and Product-Centered Intersections

A clear theme with these teacher-directors is that they use both process-centered and product-centered activities as they progress through rehearsals toward performance. In the true sense of the theatre as a laboratory for applying skills and knowledge, the rehearsals are times of exploration, experimentation, and discovery. Both students and director engage in critical thinking and decision making. Utilizing theatre games, improvisations, drama techniques, field research, art, music, and movement, they reach decisions about text and character interpretation, business, and staging choices. Design and tech students are engaged in early rehearsals and are in leadership roles collaboratively making and implementing production decisions. As in Kent's story at the beginning of this section, the production environment these directors create with young people is one of a nurturing classroom and a workshop imbued with the rigors of the theatre. Unlike productions in which unguided actors are left to flounder or where directors impose every choice, learner-centered teachers' shared production processes yield investment, ownership, and performances of great depth, interest, and vibrancy.

Viola Spolin (1983) is a pioneer still ahead of her time. Her writings and her work with improvisation continue to inspire, challenge, and liberate performance from dogma and tradition. As improvisation is embedded into exploration of text, theme, character, and the relation of these to students' lives, young people find their authentic voices and power as performers. Here Spolin speaks clearly about the relationship between process and product:

It stands to reason that if we direct all our efforts toward reaching a goal, we stand in grave danger of losing everything on which we have based our daily activities. For when a goal is superimposed on an activity instead of evolving out of it, we often feel cheated when we reach it.

> In order to approach the theatre as artists, we should have a good look at our tools and how we make decisions. How do we approach one another in the arena of a rehearsal or on a stage? How do we begin, how do we proceed, and what are our allies?
>
> —Anne Bogart

When the goal appears easily and naturally and comes from growth rather than forcing, the end-result, performance or whatever, will be no different from the process that achieved the result. . . . How much more certain would knowledge be if it came from and out of the excitement of learning itself. (26)

If it is true that thought has meaning only when generated by action upon the world, the subordination of students to teachers becomes impossible.

—PAULO FREIRE, EDUCATOR AND AUTHOR

Blending process and product to accommodate students' diverse learning styles requires a flexible style of directing. These teachers make adjustments in their directing style throughout the rehearsal process, and even within each rehearsal, to keep the process learner-centered.

In any given production, a director may find the need to move back and forth along a continuum from a director- or process-centered approach to a learner- or product-centered one, based on students' experience, skills, and their greater or lesser ability to engage in the collaborative process on a given text. (See Figure 2–4.) As anyone who has directed knows, there are an enormous number of decisions of varying magnitudes that must be made when mounting a show. Inviting all company members to make each decision is ludicrous, time consuming, and impractical. Wisdom and balance are needed to determine which decisions will promote students' growth as artists and individuals. Learner-centered teacher-artists are masters at finding decisions that empower each student. This ability seems to come from keen observation, intuition, patience, practice, and a willingness to make a mistake or two along the way. The attention to individual students' needs helps each one grow as a young person and a young artist.

Learning from my mistakes has helped me grow as an artist and teacher. There have been times in the past when I was teaching high school or doing a youth theatre piece that I got so into my process that I almost lost sight of the students. We would be brainstorming lots of ideas, interpretations, and staging choices for

> I used to block everything. Then I got more courage. I stopped writing the blocking on my script. . . . I try to know what the kernel of the scene is. . . . The embodiment I more or less work out with the actors.
>
> —Zelda Fichlander

Figure 2–4   **A Continuum of Directing Practices**

Director-Centered Practice				Learner-Centered Practice
The director has all the answers and often tells students what to do, how, and when.	The director invites feedback on his/her ideas from selected students at selected times.	The director includes students in decision-making process. Final decisions are made by the director.	Students and director make decisions collaborately.	Students make all decisions and invite teacher input.

Figure 2–5 *Those who make theatre with secondary school students must be both artists and teachers.*

Work with the student where he is, not where you think he should be.

—*Viola Spolin*

a given scene. I wanted them to make *a lot* of the decisions. Some actors loved experimenting and were happy to go home, make choices, and come to the next rehearsal ready to share. Others would look at me bewildered and confused, struggling for the "right" answer. I had overwhelmed them. They were scared and uncertain, but I had mistaken their silence for contemplation. They were unused to voicing their opinions or exploring different options and I hadn't created a way for them to tell me of their discomfort during *my* process. I hadn't explained that the actor's art involves generating choices and making decisions. I was so taken with my collaborative directing process that I had missed the fact that we weren't collaborating. We hadn't made this *our* process.

After recognizing this problem, I shifted my directing style, limiting the number and nature of decisions I was asking each student to make. This made the work safer for them. I offered them a suggestion as a starting point: "How about beginning this first moment sitting at the kitchen table." If they looked uncomfortable after trying it, I might ask where else their character might be at that moment. I would also frame choices, giving them options. Referring to them by their character names I would say, "Would you be fixing a meal or doing the dishes at this point?" Sometimes they would come up with another alternative and we would grow the scene from there. Active decision making got them away from acting in their heads, analyzing every choice, and instead got them into their bodies, moving and playing each moment intuitively and kinesthetically. I also scheduled shorter rehearsals with them, used more theatre games, improvisations, and ensemble activities, and I included more experienced students in rehearsals who could model decision-making and explorative work. At first I asked them to do less on their own outside of rehearsals. Eventually they became the veterans modeling collaboration.

Fursey Gotuaco talks about how learner-centered production work frees students to be decision makers.

> I've [seen] how much more mature [my students] are because they've had so many . . . opportunities to make decisions and see how their decisions impact a wider circle of people around them. . . . Each show has a [student] technical director and designers. . . . They . . . work directly with the crew heads who decide everything that they need and how they can create it under budget. . . . They've got to figure out "How can I motivate [crew members] to work . . . without losing the friendship?" And for . . . them . . . power and authority . . . [is] kind of new. And . . . they've got to learn how to give and take criticism. . . . And . . . when they hit a snag . . . it's reality. It's a real problem that they've got to solve. (2002)

Patsy Koch Johns, who teaches in Lincoln, Nebraska, captures the spirit that is at the heart of this approach to theatre making.

> Theatre is collaborative. . . . It takes a director to control and orchestrate . . . but if that control becomes too egocentric, then . . . I don't think the art evolves in the right way. And the power of many is certainly more powerful artistically than the power of one. . . . Maybe that's why theatre is so amazing to people. . . . Maybe our amazement comes from the fact that it comes from many. I don't have to stand alone. . . . It's not a lonely art. (2002)

The power and joy that comes from theatrical collaboration with young people is a theme that emerged often in my conversations with teachers.

Artistic Standards in a Learner-Centered Program

Stanislavski is credited with saying something to the effect of "There *is* a difference between theatre for adults and theatre for children. Theatre for children should be better." There *should* be high artistic standards for theatre with young performers. How many of us cringe to hear, "That was a terrific *high school* play" or "That was a great job for *middle school kids*." These comments create a second class of theatre and provide a justification for poor-quality work. Many teachers look at these comments not as compliments but as excuses for work that isn't fully realized or is otherwise ill-suited to the company. Theatre is theatre. It either is compelling, entertaining, meaningful, or it isn't. This is not to say that we—like so many others who earn their living as directors—haven't had our share of glorious failures. It means that we don't have a different artistic standard just because our company members are kids.

Part of the problem is the kind of plays some directors choose to produce with young people. While the selection of dramatic material is discussed at length in Chapter 3, it is appropriate here to point out how poor play selection can

Figure 2–6 *A high school production of* **The Secret Garden.**

perpetuate a culture of "high-school theatre" and low artistic standards. When directors deliberately use inexperienced student-artists, limited facilities, and small budgets to produce plays created originally for Broadway, they are often setting students up to fail. Even if plays from Broadway and the regional theatre repertoire are developmentally appropriate for students to see and perform, we must carefully assess our skills, our students' needs, and our human and material resources before launching into production. The question to ask is not "How can I do this play?" but "How can producing this play be both an artful and learner-centered experience for all involved?"

It is also an issue of how we approach the plays we choose to direct. Children never benefit when we lower or limit our expectations of them. Learner-centered directors have committed themselves to helping students define and meet high standards. They are problem solvers and solution finders who develop and improvise techniques that stretch their own artistry and enable students to learn the crafts of theatre making. Their rehearsals are learning laboratories where, for example, students can discover effective uses of their bodies and voices as well as tools for developing compelling scenes and characters. These teachers regularly see other directors' work, attend classes and workshops, and adopt new techniques.

When we talk about artistic standards for theatre with young people, questions about appropriate critical response to their work arise. Post-performance feedback sessions can be occasions where classmates or audience members intersperse a few positive remarks with comments like "Well, *I* would have done it this way." or "I didn't get it." or "Why did you put her in *that* dress?"

Liz Lerman is a performer, choreographer, educator, and founder of Liz Lerman Dance Exchange. She has evolved an artist-centered approach to criticism that makes audience response an opportunity for dialogue and an exchange grounded in mutual respect. Her four-step approach is equally effective for classroom performances, rehearsal feedback, and post-show talk-back sessions (Lerman and Borstel 2003).

Lerman's process involves first inviting statements of meaning from responders ("What was stimulating, surprising, challenging, meaningful for you?") (19). This is followed by focused questions about the work posed to responders by the artists themselves (19–20). After a discussion of these questions, responders ask the artists informational or factual questions in a neutral manner.

> Instead of saying, "It's too long" (an opinion) or "Why are your pieces always so long?" (a question that couches an opinion) a person might ask "What were you trying to accomplish in the final section?" or "Tell me the most important ideas you want us to get and where is that happening in this piece?" . . . The actual process of trying to form opinions into neutral questions enables the responder to recognize and acknowledge the personal values at play. Often these are the very questions that the artist needs to hear. (Lerman and Borstel 2003, 20–21, 23)

The last step in the process is to share opinions by permission. Permissioned opinions follow a protocol that allows the artist to retain control of what is shared.

> Responders first name the topic of the opinion and ask the artist for permission to state it. For instance, "I have an opinion about the costumes. Do you want to hear it?"
>
> In response, the artist has the option to say "yes" or "no." The artist may have several reasons for not wanting to hear the opinion: Perhaps he has already heard enough opinions about the costumes and wants to move to something else; perhaps he is very interested in hearing about the costumes, but not from that responder, or perhaps the opinion is irrelevant because . . . the costumes used for the showing have nothing to do with those planned for the ultimate presentation. . . . In most cases, however, the artist will say "yes" because the process has laid the ground work for this moment. (Lerman and Borstel 2003, 22)

I have been involved in this process as an artist and as a responder. I have adapted it for use in my college classes and I encourage my student teachers to use it in their work. This approach can change critical response experiences from "bloodletting sessions" to opportunities for communication and understanding. Ultimately, this leads to better art and better insight into others' artistic processes.

VOICES FROM THE FIELD

Dave Barnes (2002) and Donna Barnes (2002) both teach in Illinois at Oswego High School. Together they have created a familylike atmosphere within their theatre program. Alumni from years past continue to return to the school to support the program. Dave and Donna nurture each student and build self-esteem while setting and meeting high standards in all aspects of the program. Here is an excerpt from their theatre handbook.

> The Theatre Department at Oswego High School is designed to assist students in discovering the joys of theatre while maintaining a high quality of production. Students who desire to be involved in the program should understand that while theatre can be a lot of fun, it also involves discipline and an understanding of the need to work toward quality.
>
> - At this high school we do *NOT* produce "High School Theatre."
> - We produce quality theatre performed by high school students.
>
> The preceding statements . . . describe two different sets of attitudes about high school theatre. The first sentence describes productions where the feeling is, "Well what did you expect? They're just high school kids." The thought is an expression of mediocrity and inferior theatre. The second sentence states an attitude of professionalism. . . . The constant striving for excellence results in quality theatre and an exciting experience for all concerned. (Barnes, Dave 1999, 1)

Intersections Between Classroom Work and Production Work

A learner-centered approach to theatre *must* be part of both classroom instruction *and* the production process. Many teachers I interviewed make conscious connections between work in their theatre classrooms and work in their production "laboratory," their after-school theatre programs. While all produce plays, some teachers have production classes solely for making these connections. Some have one theatre class or a sequential curriculum of theatre classes. Whatever the individual configuration of productions and classes, these people recognize that they are always teaching. They situate themselves comfortably in the role of teacher-artist and encourage their pupils to view themselves as student-artists. To unify their programs, they incorporate improvisation and acting exercises, research, design, theatre technology, audition techniques, stage management, rehearsal etiquette, and work with text, voice, and movement into classes *and* rehearsals.

Blending performance and learning can have other benefits. Rick Garcia mounts a production with each of his high school theatre classes. He varies the kind of work produced to accommodate the skills and interests of the students in each class. For beginning-level students, many of whom have limited English skills, he uses "Talk Theatre." Students write personal narratives and Rick works with them individually and collectively to produce an original performance of their poems, monologues, and scenes. This approach encourages students to find their voices and share them with others. Rick has found this a particularly effective approach in classes where students are academically challenged, feel marginalized, apathetic, ambivalent, or reluctant to participate in school. With other students, Rick works in small increments. He will coach some students one-on-one, moving them from one line of dialogue spoken while sitting by Rick's desk to a fully performed monologue from one of Shakespeare's plays. In this way, Rick reaches each child along a fluid process-product continuum (Garcia 2002).

The creative melding of curriculum and performance also allows students to apply their knowledge and skills in wider circles of influence. A teacher from the state of Washington, for example, developed a theatre-in-education (TIE) class for her high school students. Students devise interactive theatre pieces about topics of concern to them. They then work as actor-teachers, touring their pieces to area schools, engaging audience members in and out of role, and facilitating dialogue about the issues raised in the play. Teachers like Sandy DiMartino and Steve Bogart regularly devise plays in their classes to foster conversations about social change with school and public audiences (Bogart 2003a and b, DiMartino 2003).

Given the state of theatre education nationally (see preceding Chapter 1), these teachers are the exception. The link between curricular and cocurricular work is not the norm. Emphasis and value is often still placed on productions. In more and more schools, however, the days are gone when being a great director and winning the one-act play contest can compensate for poorly managed classrooms and programs focused on productions that serve only the most talented students. This is not to say that those engaged in best practice aren't concerned with or don't value performances of the highest quality. It means that because our performers are *students*, *we* must be both skilled artists *and* skilled teachers. Teacher-directors must select dramatic material and classroom and rehearsal activities that help students develop as artists *and* as human beings. Best practice directors are knowledgeable about theatre, contemporary directing practices, *and* how to teach. They know how to best engage and teach a range of young people while producing high-quality theatre.

Producing Students' Work in a Learner-Centered Program

Generating or producing original performance pieces with students is a common element of best practice (see page 10). Some teachers devise original plays with students using what has been called "collective creation" (Lang 2002). Others teach playwrighting, or their students participate in young playwrights events. Some students create work independently or in small groups as part of a class, festival, or school showcase of student work. Teachers also commission artists-in-residence to write plays for their students or to partner with students in the development of a new piece. (Partnerships between schools and local artists are discussed further in Chapter 5.)

Questions about artistic quality and appropriate critical response often arise with production of new works with and by students. How does a teacher engaged in learner-centered practice address these questions?

The pressures to play "Beat the Clock" when devising or developing new material for the stage can tempt us to sacrifice artistic quality and elements of learner-centered practice. As playwright James Still commented during a recent visit to The University of Texas at Austin, "There is never enough time. Even if we had twice as long, it wouldn't be enough time" (Still 2003). His point was that at the very outset we need to acknowledge that there will never be enough time, so plan accordingly. Original work requires considerable organization, flexibility, and great discipline so students can move successfully through the development and production processes within the time available. This requires negotiation throughout the process regarding who makes what decisions, when, and how the company will handle the inevitable feeling that "We need more time!"

There are other challenges to consider and respond to when creating original work with students using a learner-centered approach. In her article "Collaborative Creativity in a High School Drama Class," Debra McLauchlan comments on the need for balance between students' freedom and teacher-imposed structure. Speaking about a class play project, she writes, "Direct teacher intervention sometimes provoked either silent hostility or withdrawal of commitment. A more positive approach was a negotiated effort to bridge differences." She also identifies the need for a "sense of shared identity" and that "[a]greement on common goals provided the most productive basis for conflict resolution" (2001, 55).

Working for a balance of freedom and structure can directly affect the artistic quality of original or student-devised work. How do we develop work with or by young people that allows them to voice their concerns and interests but also allows them to look at their work critically? This can be a slippery slope in a learner-centered program. Original works are often deeply personal expressions by the artists and can pose special challenges for directors devising work with emerging adolescents. Interactions must allow students freedom of expression while also helping them develop their own aesthetics in relation to the range of critical standards in our field. The following incident illustrates the need for a balance of freedom and structure.

Theatre teacher Roxanne Schroeder-Arce annually produces *VOICE*, a showcase of student written work. A student playwright whose work was included in the showcase had told actors to add some unrehearsed, sexually explicit material for the first evening's performance. After seeing the performance, Roxanne reminded him that no unrehearsed material was to be performed because it is unfair to those who must call cues and perform in the play. She stressed that this rule had been discussed during the production process. She made clear that only work that had been refined, rehearsed, and of predictable artistic merit was to be performed. During the second performance, the student again added unrehearsed material. With actors still performing, Roxanne asked the stage manager to call the cast for the next piece to "places" and to cue the lights for a cross-fade into that play. Afterward there was a heated confrontation by a group of students who felt the playwright had been censored (2002b).

In this incident, social, educational, and even moral implications of encouraging student-developed work came to light. For Roxanne, it was not a censorship issue; the fact that the unrehearsed material was sexually explicit was not the discussion point. Instead she focused on the guidelines for appropriate theatre practice that they had all agreed upon. The guidelines needed to be upheld. A discussion was held later and students talked about their feelings; some students expressed gratitude that she was adhering to the rules, and the situation was resolved after conversations took place with all involved.

It is interesting to note that when this student playwright learned that Roxanne was moving to a position in another state, he was the most vocal about the future of the program, especially the playwrighting project. He wondered who would carry on the showcase and encourage students to express themselves in the important way Roxanne had done in *VOICE*. He had realized that art comes with both freedom and responsibility and is something to be valued.

In devising work with young performers, we consider and think critically about whatever personal ideas emerge. We then use movement, improvisation, text exploration, and revision techniques to lift what might be self-indulgent contemplations, moderately humorous stories, or a venting of adolescent angst to

> I utilize as much of an actor's contribution (or a designer's) as I can, and edit out the rest. I am the organizer of others' impulses.
>
> —Mark Lamos

a level where the images and ideas resonate for audience members and are stageworthy and artful. Ideas for developing work with young artists and selected rehearsal strategies are included at the end of this chapter.

Time Investment in a Learner-Centered Program

This emphasis on learner-centered production work will require more rehearsal time *at the outset* than in a more traditional "read, block, and run" model. As interactive process work leads to product, however, directors are saved a lot of time and frustration. During the last, sometimes hectic, days of rehearsals, learner-centered directors are working with an ensemble who owns their production. The students understand and assume their artistic and social responsibilities to the play and to the cast. They are able to add nuances and make needed adjustments in timing and tempo to artfully "tell the story" they collectively created.

Teaching and directing from a learner-centered standpoint means "front-loading" the labor intensive aspects early in the production process. Investing time in assessing students' skills, learning styles, intelligences, interests and knowledge at the beginning of the process enables teacher-directors to frame objectives and design lessons or rehearsal plans that maximize students opportunities for success throughout the process. Changes in teaching style and directing practices require a *different* use of time, but ultimately not more time. Helping students learn strategies for making their own acting, design, technical, or dramaturgical choices at the beginning of rehearsals means directors are not spending time during tech week reminding students of their blocking and lines, having beat-the-clock crew calls, or doing lobby displays alone. If teachers are sharing decisions, and students are becoming increasingly self-directed and engaged, then the teacher is spending less time giving orders and directions and more time being a facilitator and resource for learning. This approach enables students to feel the power of self-discovery as well as the consequences of neglected responsibilities.

In learner-centered programs, students create and drive a community where knowledge is shared, passed along to the next generation, and deepened. These are programs that relieve the teacher of the burden of micro-management and the drudgery of constantly having to reteach how to call cues, how to operate the light board, and that it's OK to make an acting choice or have an opinion about blocking.

> [My teacher] works with you on how to identify with your character. . . . She'll work with you one-on-one. She just takes a lot of time for that.
> —*High School Theatre Student*

An Example of Learner-Centered Practice in the Classroom

"The Spot" by Bill Hansen

Bill Hansen (2002) teaches Stagecraft, Great Plays, Group Problem Solving, Acting, Directing, and Playwriting at Lincoln High School in Manitowoc, Wisconsin. He directs and is the technical director for all of the shows. He also stage manages the 800-seat theatre when it is used for other events. "The Spot" is a series of exercises he uses in the classroom to build ensemble and an awareness of composition and focus on stage.

NOTES ABOUT "THE SPOT"

I first experienced the basic form of this exercise at [a summer intensive] for teachers with [a guest artist] from Wales. "The Spot" is (1) an exercise, and (2) a tool. As an *exercise*, keep expanding the students' use of body, voice, and imagination. Add more difficulty for the group or individuals to keep it interesting. The exercises serve as rehearsal *tools* as they become part of a shared language.

HOW TO PLAY

The teacher selects a spot on the floor and each player observes five simple rules:

- Play silently.
- Avoid physical contact with others.
- Move freely about the playing space.
- Enter the spot and take focus as often as you wish.
- The game ends when all have taken the spot at least once. (Then players all sit down.)

To take focus, one at a time students proceed to the spot, stop moving, and act as if a string, attached to their upper chest, is raising them up (not tiptoe, just a posture change). When any person takes the spot, they are asking for focus. They stay frozen until they wish to release focus, which is only after they have everyone's focus. Performers must give focus by freezing all movement and looking at the person on the spot.

To release focus, the student on the spot drops the body posture and moves off of the spot.

VARIATIONS The following variations to "The Spot" can be played with the whole group and then two groups. Variations can be used in any order appropriate to the group, class content, or rehearsal needs. Reflection and discussion about what students noticed, experienced, were surprised by, and so forth, can be incorporated as well.

- Change movement of the group to specific activities.
- Change the spot elevation by using a box, chair, platform, or ladder.
- Change the spot to a specific change in posture, still frozen.
- Change the spot to a sound with a person making the sound while frozen, and repeating the sound until releasing focus (still a silent activity except for the person asking for focus).

- Change from silence to gibberish or talking except for the person taking the spot, who becomes silent, followed by everyone else.
- Change and let the person taking the spot keep talking, but all must be quiet until the spot is released.
- Change to two different groups within the same space, only giving and taking focus from or with members in your own group and paying no attention to those in the other group. (Use two different spots to start and, when mastered, use only one spot.)

Students can then move to physical contact. Start by changing the spot to a person who is pointed at. That person takes focus, freezes and points at another player. Other players must freeze and give focus to the person being pointed at. The person pointed at freezes and makes eye contact with the person pointing. The person taking focus is demanding focus from one other person. All are released when the pointing stops. Vocally this can be done with "you" shouted or whispered and eye contact made without pointing. The variations can be combined as needed.

Using "The Spot" with theatre students has several benefits:

- Students learn about giving and taking focus in every scene: In a rehearsal, ask why characters are giving or taking focus; invite students to try different staging ideas to create focus.
- By using this exercise, audiences can tell where they are to look at any given moment in large crowd scenes.
- Since students share a common vocabulary, solving problems in a show becomes much easier and quicker. (Hansen 2003)

Examples of Learner-Centered Practice in Production

Choices *Directorial Journal by Diane Stewart*

Diane Stewart (2003) was teaching at Cypress Lake High School Center for the Arts in Fort Myers, Florida when she ventured into an amazing journey of learner-centered practice. The following are excerpts from Diane's Directorial Journal for her production of *Choices*. This original theatre piece explores resistance to the use of alternative treatments for the healing of cancer and is based on experiences with her husband, Ken.

This project was part of Diane's MFA in Directing received through a distance learning program at the University of Utah. Diane spent summers in Salt Lake City. She worked on campus and at the Sundance Festival with directors such as Moises Kaufman. Throughout the year she participated in online instruction with university faculty who then mentored the teachers in their own schools (Dynak

2002, Lindahl 2002b, Stewart 2002). These brief excerpts from Diane's early rehearsal process are a glimpse of the leanered-centered directing style she used to guide the company through this provocative play.

Wednesday, December 06, 2000
I was so nervous about today that I planned [enough to do] for about three days.

Thursday, December 07, 2000
I began with listing the strengths of yesterday's work, then asked for additions from the cast.

Wednesday, December 13, 2000
The cast asked why I had not assigned the small ensemble roles. I said I wanted to play around with [that] more, but they convinced me that they could do better work if they knew a role was assigned to them. I said I will cast these before the next rehearsal.

Ken was here for this rehearsal. . . . . I had introduced him at the beginning of the rehearsal. . . . The kids asked Ken a lot of questions about his cancer experience. Many of them shared stories of relatives' experiences. . . . We broke at 4:30, but several students stayed much longer and asked Ken a lot of questions. I came away from this rehearsal feeling very positive.

Thursday, January 04, 2001
Continued discussion from yesterday [and what students thought the play was about]. I proposed: "[This is] . . . a play about responsibility. What does that mean to you?" More discussion followed and the . . . consensus was that this play is about *accepting responsibility for your own choices.*

Activity: Divide into . . . [three] groups. . . . Begin to create the [characters'] group memories. How do [you] know each other? When did [you] meet? What are [your] common experiences? . . . Where is [your] office/house? What does it look like?

Assignment for Monday: Create an autobiography for your character. Come prepared to enter into improvs to create your past experiences.

Monday, January 08, 2001
Since I had a faculty meeting, I gave the actors the task of discussing their characters together until I returned. Bad idea—I should have given them more specific directions or questions or improvs to play out. I discovered that they had not done their homework—and I don't mean that they hadn't thought about their characters. The answers they were giving to my questions did not match some of the givens [give circumstances] in the text. . . . We read over three scenes to talk about character . . . I asked them all to go back to the text and comb it for givens.

Thursday, January 18
Rehearsal called for Emily and Chorus #s 1–6 for the flashback scene [that] we call "Cancer Journey." . . . Our goal was to experiment with the feeling, mood and staging of the scene.

First we discussed who the [Chorus] characters are or what they represent. The cast felt that [#s 2–5] represented doctors. [Chorus] #1 and #6 were proponents of traditional and nontraditional medicine, respectively. We read the scene twice and discussed the therapies and ideas mentioned. Then I asked them what the scene looks like in their heads . . . a metaphor. Some suggested by me were a tornado, nightmare, a bombing, a point-counterpoint. They suggested a courtroom cross-examination and a debate. We decided we liked the debate image, but with the feel that one side was heavily favored or winning.

I asked them to make a tableau of the beginning of the scene. They set themselves up around the periphery of the space. All were standing except one, who chose to sit, with Emily standing in the center. They all knew it didn't look right for the one person to be sitting, so he stood. They described Emily as a pinball getting "bounced" around by ideas. I thought this was a good image, so I said "Hold onto it for a minute. Make a tableau of what the end of the scene looks like." They created a wall of bodies of all the traditional doctors. Emily was in front of the wall, and the one lone alternative doctor was on her other side with hand outstretched. Emily was looking over her shoulder at the wall, but leaning toward the lone doctor. It was a powerful tableau and they all loved it.

So, now what happens in between the two tableaux? I told them to take the first tableau position. I was going to count to ten and they should move through the scene (no text) and end up at the end tableau. They did and the most interesting part was that #1 and #6 started to face off as in a debate with Emily between them and the others sort of moving around them. We worked this over and over about six times. The cast always knew it wasn't right before I gave that opinion. The flow wasn't working. We tried clockwise movement and random crossing but it wasn't right.

Only three of the actors present today have had [Anne Bogart's] Viewpoints training, but all of a sudden one of them said we needed to define the *topography*! They felt that the circular and random patterns that #s 2–5 were moving in were too "soft." So we tried it again, and I told them to walk like they were on graph paper and could only make ninety-degree turns. It began to work. The whole feel of the scene changed. I was so excited! I had to stop for a minute and tell them how proud I was that they could work like this. They expressed how much more fun this was than being told when to cross and on what line! I have one boy in the cast who often just goes for the laugh in class and *never* makes suggestions. [In this] he was so creative— suggesting all sorts of things!

After a few more tries, we were able to rough out the movement patterns that really worked. We picked up the text now and tried the movement and text together. The images of a bombing and a debate got sort of fused. I think it works! I left very excited and so did the cast.

I have to say that I think Anne Bogart is really on to something when she says she often doesn't know what she is going to say when she gets up off her stool and walks into the playing space to make comments. She often gets an idea on the walk! I have been pushing myself to try this for I know I am too much the planner! I have goals for the rehearsal and some ideas in my head of what I want the scene to look like. I have a picture in my head, but now I am trying to let the actors experiment with their own pictures. They are young, but they are so creative. They have much better ideas than I have sometimes. Letting go is scary but really fun. I mean letting go of my need to plan.

Each actor is different. To unlock his or her special gifts is the director's main goal during the rehearsal process.

—Mark Lamos

Planning means I will be safe and nothing will go wrong. I will be able to finish six pages of blocking in the allotted time. And planning often means there have been no creative risks taken. Working this way is slower, but the payoff is bigger! (Stewart 2003)

"Moment Analysis" by Brian Hall

[I am] . . . trying different things that are out of the norm and out of [my] comfort zone, trying to get kids to think out of the box and help them understand that theatre has a more important role in our culture than just going to see a musical and then going home and not talking about it or thinking about it.
—*Brianna Lindahl*, Teacher

Brian Hall has taught for thirty years and directed more than 130 plays and musicals in his career. He had his own professional musical theatre company and worked as an artist-in-residence throughout Arizona. Brian now teaches secondary school in the Phoenix Valley and works as a freelance director. He is also an adjunct faculty member at Arizona State University.

During rehearsals and in the classroom, Brian uses an approach that he has developed called Moment Analysis. Moment analyses are done after ensemble work with the company and after initial explorations of the text. Using this method, Brian works alongside performers as *they* make choices regarding text interpretation, staging, business, character development, character interaction, and pacing. Performers collaborate with him and create a "road map" of well-crafted, aesthetically pleasing moments. His approach has proven highly effective for inexperienced performers as well as seasoned professionals.

Brian suggests beginning slowly, with one or two solo numbers from a musical, an important series of moments from a text, or one scene.[3] As directors and performers grow familiar with the approach, students can work independently and the strategies can be extended to an entire production. Directors and performers are surprised how quickly this work grows and how rich the performances are once everyone feels the freedom and excitement of rehearsing this way. Once the structure is explored, the work takes on an ease and naturalness and builds in texture, intricacy, and freshness.

SAMPLE MOMENT ANALYSIS OF A MUSICAL NUMBER

STEP ONE: DIVIDE THE SONG TEXT INTO MOMENTS AND LIST THEM   A play or musical unfolds to an audience moment by moment, like beads being strung on a necklace. Each moment conveys meaning about characters, places, and events. Collectively, these moments form the story being told. Performers and director must therefore craft each moment to tell the story and convey the dramatic truth of the play.

It is very important to create an atmosphere for actors that is conducive to their doing a great deal of the work . . . I really do believe that the work is a collaboration . . . that the actors absolutely have the right to experiment and fail.
—*Gordon Davidson*

A moment is *the smallest single action of a play*. It is smaller than a beat, as we know it in theatre. A moment may be a line of dialogue, a phrase, a single word, a silent thought, a light change, a chord, or a movement.

To begin moment analysis, start with the following steps:

- On a printed edition of the song text (lyrics), have performers write parenthesis around words to distinguish between the *moments*.

- On a separate piece of paper, have them write the song text (lyrics) with one moment on each line, like a *list*.

Sample Text

"Somewhere, over the rainbow, way up high, there's a land that I heard of once in a lullaby."

Moments
(Somewhere) (over the rainbow) (way up high) (there's a land that I heard of) (once) (in a lullaby.)

List of Moments
Somewhere
over the rainbow
way up high
there's a land that I heard of
once
in a lullaby.

Ask performers to speak aloud the text inserting a slightly perceptible pause between each moment. Have students compare their interpretation with someone else's. Evaluate the choices and/or differences among the different versions. Where does a moment feel too long? Could it be divided into two or more moments? When is a moment too short? Allow multiple interpretations.

STEP TWO: USE QUESTIONS TO HELP PERFORMERS INTERPRET AND STAGE THE TEXT. Both you and the performer share the quest for the interpretation of the text. Questions focus the performer's concentration, memory, and artistic skills and put most of the responsibility to solve each task on the performer. Occasionally, to keep the process moving, and so you don't overwhelm the performer, you may want to offer a couple of possible answers and allow the performer to try one or more.

A moment analysis calls for a *series* of questions posed to the performer for *each* moment of the text being staged. Students can modify their text division as you work. Allow performers to experiment rather than jumping to "the right answer." One of the joys of the process is that oftentimes new moments appear out of nowhere as the performer is working.

Work from the first moment and move in order through the moments to allow performers to internalize the text sequence. The order and number of questions can vary depending on the students, the complexity of the text with which you are working, and the rehearsal schedule.

Questions are posed to the *character*, not the actor. Work in an inquiry mode or wondering mode rather than an answer-driven mode. Responses given to questions should be based on the text and first given by the performer orally, not written. The first set of questions should be asked while discussing the text with actors "at the table." Each question is answered *for each moment* listed in Step One.

> Tying the imagination to the action is the key. And that's where the director becomes so important in helping the actor find the right physical action so that, as the character, he can rely upon doing that action every night.
>
> —*Mark Lamos*, Director

"At the Table" Moment Analysis Questions

- What is the situation? Briefly discuss what is happening and what just happened.

- Is this something the character is experiencing internally or externally?

- Is this a real or imagined moment? Is it grounded in reality, the imagination, or fantasy?

- What is the time frame? Has time stopped? Is it racing, sluggish, or real time? (See Figure 2–8.)

The second set of questions performers should explore "on their feet." This is *not* table work, but an active, *experiential* step for the performer. Performers explore several possible choices for each question. Once a choice has been explored and then settled on (although these remain fluid), the performer can move on to the next question for that same moment or follow that same question through ten or fifteen consecutive moments. Some performers need this latter approach so they feel the flow of the text.

Figure 2–7 *Rich, textured performances result from learner-centered moment analysis work.* **(Bradford High School production of Once On This Island)**

Figure 2–8 *"At the Table" Moment Analysis Questions*

TEXT	SITUATION	INTERNAL/EXTERNAL?	IMAGINED/REAL?	TIME FRAME?
Somewhere	I was just dismissed by Auntie Em. A tornado is coming. Nobody understands me.	internal	real	time stopped (for whole piece)
over the rainbow	I am yearning for excitement and understanding.	external	imagined	same
way up high	I want to escape from here.	external	imagined	same
there's a land that I heard of	I am trying to remember something.	internal	real	same
once	I am recalling a brief moment of my childhood with my mother.	internal	real	same
in a lullaby	I am remembering my only memory of my mother.	internal	real	same

"On Your Feet" Moments Analysis Questions

- What are you (the character) doing? (action, answered with a verb based on the text [*not* the actor's blocking])
- To whom/what are you speaking? (answered, e.g., myself, over the rainbow, the world, my past, mom)
- Where is this to be imaged? (answered with one of eight circles, see Figure 2–10 and page 53)
- What is your attitude? (answered with an adverb)
- What are you feeling? (answered with an adjective, adverb, or verb)
- Are you sitting, standing, kneeling, or lying down? (answer with a verb)
- Should you move? (answered yes or no)
- Where should you move? (answered)
- What's the dramatic truth of this moment? (answered briefly)

With some performers or pieces a few of these questions will be sufficient to realize the piece. Under other circumstances, you will want to use all of the questions. Use only those that will help you and the performers create a meaningful performance and use them in the order you think will be most helpful to performers (see Figure 2–9). (Note: Two of the questions, "To whom/what are you speaking?" and "Where is this to be imaged?" are discussed further on page 53.)

SKILL DIRECTIONS   It may be necessary to offer performers skill directions during this step. Skill directions are open-ended and help you and the performer get going in the same direction immediately. The performer must work to solve the task, but doesn't have to take as much responsibility for the interpretation as a whole. As performers work, insert skill directions to heighten or make a moment more specific, to break a moment into smaller moments, and to cull from the text more of the dramatic truth of moments.

Skill directions are unavoidable, but try to use them sparingly at the start, and more for polish. Though they are effective and specific, you are still acting like the proverbial traffic cop telling the performer what to do and how to interpret, and since you chose the directions, it is probable that performers may not retain any rationale for them. The educational value, therefore, is less than with questions. Examples of skill directions you might use as performers work though a moment include:

Image [that]
hear [that]
internalize more
mime [that]
see [that]
move more (or less)
gesture with [your hand, head]
play that bigger

Directors might be tempted to ask questions that are vague, often director-centered, or even reader-, audience-, or critic-centered rather than learner-centered, action-based, or "actable." With poor questions like these, performers can stall or feel like they must mind-read to please you or must come up with the "right" answers. In this case, the director and performer do *not* succeed in going forward together most of the time. They beat around the bush together. This is taking the character to the analyst's couch. The performer ends up paraphrasing the play, the text, the moment or ends up discussing feelings, actions, words, or thoughts that occur later in the play's time. Vague questions result in vague interpretations. Some examples of vague questions include:

Who are you?
What's your motivation?
Why did you do that?
Why did you gesture?
Where's your focus?

> Structure gives a framework to proceed on. The creative work of the performers often takes flight merely as a result of beginning with a moment structure. The question, 'what do I do' or 'how do I begin' need never be heard again!
>
> —Brian Hall

Figure 2–10 **Sample Moment Analysis: Over the Rainbow**

TEXT	SITUATION?	INTERNAL/ EXTERNAL?	IMAGINED/ REAL	TIME FRAME?	WHAT ARE YOU DOING? ACTION	SPEAKING TO?	CIRLES	HOW? (ATTITUDE)	FEELING?	POSITION/ MOVE?	WHERE?	DRAMATIC TRUTH?
Some-where	Just dismissed by Auntie Em/Tornado coming/Nobody under-stands me	internal	real	time stopped	reasoning	myself	2	longingly	unful-filled	standing/no	N/A	I am growing up and I want more from life
over the rainbow	yearning for excitement and understanding	external	imagined	same	fantasizing	the world beyond the horizon	7	wistfully	same	looking out	in the direction of the audience	I want to escape this farm
way up high	I want to escape from here	same	same	same	escaping	the place where my dreams are true	7	hopeful	joyful	a couple of steps down right	where my dreams are	I'm using my fantasy to escape
there's a land that I heard of	trying to remember	internal	real	same	recalling	my memory	2	gently	comforted	no	N/A	same
once	I am recalling a brief moment of my childhood with my mother	same	same	same	remembering	my memory	1	curiously	warm	no	N/A	I am glimpsing what life was and could have been
in a lullaby	remembering	same	same	same	re-living	my memory	1	indulgently	happy/ safe	no	N/A	same

USING EIGHT CIRCLES TO PLACE IMAGES   The placement and use of images can answer most questions related to delivery: "Where do I look when I deliver this line?" "What is my relation to the audience?" "Whom do I talk to?" To image something is to use several related skills—gestures, eye focus, movement—to create an object (the rainbow) or person (my mother) that may not physically be on the stage for the audience to perceive. The imagined object or person comes to the character's mind, is remembered, is dreamed of, is imagined, is longed for, is feared, or is hated. *Where* images are visualized clearly establishes the character's state of mind, relationships, time frame, and dramatic truth.

Building on his understanding of Stanislavski's three circles of concentration, Brian employs a metaphor of eight concentric circles placed in and encircling the character. These circles can help performers answer their "Where do I look?" questions. (See Figure 2–10.) Referring to the moment analysis, performers can place internal, external, real, and imagined images to convey the dramatic truth of the piece to an audience.

STEP THREE: MARRYING THE TEXT AND THE MUSIC   For those teacher-directors working with musicals, it is important to use a learner-centered approach in all phases of the process. A song can be viewed as a duet between the character and the music. Performers should prepare the text and the music separately so they come to understand the unique contribution both the lyrics and music are making to the story being told. Remind the students that the music is their partner.

It is also important for students to realize that we learn lyrics in one part of the brain and the melody in another. Learning lyrics separately from the music allows students to understand and make informed choices about the whole song. If our students learn the lyrics and music simultaneously, they are either focusing on the lyrics and losing the melody, or they are singing notes without connecting them to the words. Students may struggle with the meaning of the lyrics or have trouble remembering them unless they hum the melody. To test this, have students say the lyrics to *The Star Spangled Banner*, with meaning, without mentally or audibly humming the melody. If students artfully can perform lyrics for their songs as monologues and can also beautifully sing the melodies independent of the words, then they are ready to put the song together and prepare for performance.

Moment analysis and music preparation occur separately but concurrently, and require collaboration and communication between the director and the musical director. (See Figure 2–11.) Once students complete their moment analysis, they are able to grow and refine each moment, blending and adjusting *their* interpretation into a fluid performance. All involved find great satisfaction in thoroughness and discovery at each step (Hall 2003b, 2003c, 1999).

Figure 2–10 *Using Eight Circles to Place Images in the Text*

Have performers imagine that they, as the character, are at the very center of an enormous eight-ring bull's eye. They then can place each image in a circle as they do their moment analysis. Choices of placement can be modified throughout rehearsals and performances.

Circle 1 *To your heart of hearts:* This circle is within you: It holds internalized places, people, objects, or ideas about which you pour your heart out, exposing your most vulnerable, true self. Your past is here. Your memory is here.

Circle 2 *To your mental self:* This circle is also within you, but is in your thoughts and mind. It holds internalized places, people, objects, or ideas about which you are thinking, worrying, having a conversation with yourself. Your past is here. Your memory is here. Your hopes and fears are here. The voice in your mind is speaking.

Circle 3 *Preciously close:* This circle includes external, precious, very closely held places, people, objects, or ideas. The images are six inches to a foot away.

Circle 4 *Within reach:* This circle includes external people, places, objects, or ideas you might grasp, reach, touch, travel or move toward, and achieve. Everything onstage near you is in this circle.

Circle 5 *Out of reach:* This circle includes external places, people, objects, or ideas at a distance just beyond the ability of your character to travel, move, touch, reach, grasp.

Circle 6 *The audience:* This circle includes places, people, objects, or ideas in the environment where the audience is. Project images and metaphorical meanings indirectly (without eye contact) into the audience's environment to include them in the scene, place, group of people, or ideas. You can use the barrier of the fourth wall metaphorically: You yearn to get out, you want to be different than you are and more like them, you want their help. For presentational style, this is also when you converse directly with the audience.

Circle 7 *The horizon:* This circle includes places, peoples, objects, or ideas large enough to encompass more of humanity than the audience. Your destiny lies here. The future lies here. Your plant-your-feet-determination is expressed to here.

Circle 8 *The universe:* This circle includes peoples, places, objects, or ideas so large as to encompass everyone and beyond. The audience feels that it occupies but a tiny fragment of a larger space. Metaphorically, places, people, and so on. assume a universal quality and importance. This is beyond the room of the performance and is larger than life.

Figure 2–11 *Marrying the Text and the Music*

Lyric Preparation	Music Preparation
Prepare and rehearse the moment analysis of the song as a monologue *without* tempo considerations.	Identify all of the vowels in the song. Sing the whole song on the vowels on perfect pitch. Take a breath between each vowel.
Look for musical moments and clues to add to the moment analysis of the lyrics. What is the music saying about time, place, mood, and images? *For example: The music may reveal a moment of realization, resignation, or a mood change by a single note or a chord. If a character is lying or having feelings they may be unaware of, this may be signaled by use of key changes or counterpoint melodies. Musical introductions can reveal if time has stopped, is moving to the past, future or is racing.* When exactly in the song text is there a key change? Where does the music modulate? At which points in the lyric does the music comment on the text by inserting a chord, note or other musical device? What is being said? Find these musical moments and place them in the moment analysis exactly where they occur in the text.	Sing the whole song syllable by syllable. Take a breath between each syllable. Don't destroy or distort vowels. Sing the whole song word by word. Breathe between each word. Add color, quality, and inflection to each word. Use pure vowels and dropped jaw.
Allow time for these moments as you continue to perform the monologue. *In Over the Rainbow, there would be a silent moment added before "Somewhere" for the music to stop time and establish what's happening for the character.*	
Adjust monologue to correct tempo. Perform with musical accompaniment *underneath*.	Sing clusters of words to create images. This is the first time to pay attention to punctuation, capital letters, and rests. Final phrasing choices are made now with longer time between breaths. Use pure vowels.
Adjust the monologue for free singing so you can partner with the music.	Free singing. *Sing on correct pitches with appropriate tempo* without *accompaniment*.
Sing monologue with accompaniment as partner.	Sing so music is fully integrated and music appears to come from the character.
Practice, adjust, and refine.	Practice, adjust, and refine.
Repeat these steps prior to each performance.	Repeat these steps prior to each performance.

Ideas for Further Reflection

Whose Program Is This?

Describe your vision of a learner-centered theatre program. Think about examples from this chapter and examples you have seen, experienced, or read about.

Consider ways in which you can sustain the best of what is present in your work and how you can change your practice to include more learner-centered activities, approaches, and principles. Reflect on the following questions:

Whose voices are shared in my classroom or performance space?

Whose voices are heard and why?

Whose voices are silenced or not heard and why?

How is power used, brokered, or shared, and by whom? Who makes what decisions?

How are students' lived experiences part of their study and practice of theatre?

Selected Resources

In addition to the works cited in this chapter, the following may offer useful ideas for further reflection.

Lazarus, Joan, and Wayne Brabender. 1997. *Theatre Arts Adventures.* St. Paul: University of Minnesota Cooperative Extension Service and 4-HCCS.
Oddey, Allison. 1996. *Devising Theatre.* New York: Routledge.
Rodgers, James W., and Wanda C. Rodgers. 1995. *Play Directors Survival Kit.* West Nyack, NY: The Center for Applied Reseach in Education.
Weigler, Will. 2001. *Strategies for Playbuilding.* Portsmouth, NH: Heinemann.

Notes

1. Margaret Wheatley's work in organizational communications led her to find the fields of quantum physics, chaos theory, and biology overturning scientific theories that had dominated the world for centuries, revealing how each large and small part of the universe operates not in conflict but in harmony, health, and beauty. Wheatley applies this understanding to her work with various groups and organizations.

2. Deb Alexander built her curriculum on the Goodrich and Hackett version of the play. Wendy Kesselman has since updated the script based on the release of Anne Frank's unedited diary.

3. Brian Hall notes that there will be more moments to analyze in musical theatre song lyrics, scenes, in poetic works, such as Shakespeare or Pinter, where the language is poetic and compressed. For other works, and many operas, there typically will be fewer moments to stage.

3   *Socially Responsible Practice*

Theatre allows us to converse with our souls, to passionately pursue and discover ways of living with ourselves and with others. We have no better way to work together, to learn about each other, to heal and to grow.

—MICHAEL ROHD

I had a junior high student say to me, "I had a dream with you in it last night, Miss D."
"Was I really me?" I said.
"Yeah. We were at a grocery store, and you looked at me and said, 'You can fly.' I said to you, 'No, Miss D., I can't fly. What are you, nuts?' And you said, 'Yes you can, just try.'"
So I had to fly through this grocery store! And I said, "Wow, I can fly up to the top of shelves and get whatever I want." And you said, "Go ahead. Take whatever you want." I said "No, I can't do that, Miss D. It's stealing." And you said . . . "I'm giving you permission. You can take whatever you want."

After he told me that, I had to go home and write it down . . . I thought . . . "This is going to be one of those stories . . . when life gets hard [that] I'm going to reread . . . and remember why I do this for a living."

—Sandra DiMartino, Teacher

I recently gained a new perspective on socially responsible practice in a seemingly odd setting—a hair salon. Discreetly placed on the counter in the salon rest room were fliers offering resources and information about domestic violence prevention. I asked the owner what made him decide to put these out. He said he had been approached by a local awareness group that told him stylists are in an ideal position to see evidence of abuse because of the nature of their regular, physical contact with clients. He arranged for his whole staff to attend a training session on recognizing domestic violence because he believes that making these resources available to staff and their clients is his responsibility. He said the significance of his action became clear to him when his sister visited the salon. She said she was grateful to see this literature available and then disclosed, for the first time, that she herself had been abused as a child. As the salon owner was talking with me I kept thinking, "He didn't *have* to take this action. He has *chosen* to do this." For him, social responsibility means recognizing the place he holds in a larger community and taking positive action to contribute to that community.

What Is Socially Responsible Theatre Education?

Almost inevitably, when I ask theatre teachers and artists this question, I receive a question in response. "What do you mean by socially responsible theatre education?" After sharing a few opinions from other teachers and artists, I ask, 'How would *you* define it?' There is usually a pause, followed by an eagerness to discuss issues in their schools and communities. They talk about problems they face and how they have responded or want to respond. They talk with conviction as individual theatre teachers and artists and as members of a larger community of educators and citizens. Most of them are endeavoring to bring about change in their own field, with their own students, school, and local communities.

Many of these teachers wish they could reach more students in their schools and use theatre more effectively to engage the school community in dialogue or action. They grapple with a desire to make a difference and they wrestle with questions about where to begin or how to continue. They face uncertainty about the impact of their efforts and concerns about how to expand, change, and diversify their programs while sustaining them at the same time. They reference their experiences and the experiences of colleagues, all the while generating as many questions as answers. For some teachers and artists, everything they do is through a lens of social responsibility and/or social engagement. For others, they offer a single project or a class in response to a specific concern.

> Kids have to make their own choices politically, philosophically, socially. I can't legislate that to them. But I can create an environment where they're empathetic in those choices. That to me is the most important idea of social responsibility.
> —Susan Morrell, Teacher

A Pattern of Awareness and Action

Looking at the experiences and steps that led these teacher-artists to their current level of socially responsible practice, I notice a cyclical pattern. These, teacher-artists:

- recognize there is a need of some kind in their school or community;
- acknowledge that theatre could be a viable and powerful tool for addressing this need, *and* that as theatre artists and teachers they are in a unique position to address this need and bring about positive change;
- identify strategies to address the need; and
- take action to effect positive change.

In *The Dreamkeepers*, Gloria Ladson-Billings succinctly characterizes the teaching practice that results from the pattern of awareness and action.

> Teachers who practice culturally relevant methods . . . believe that all of their students can succeed rather than that failure is inevitable for some. . . . They help

students make connections between their local, national, racial, cultural, and global identities. . . . Their relationships with students are fluid and equitable and extend beyond the classroom. . . . Finally, such teachers are identified by their notions of knowledge: They believe that knowledge is continuously re-created, recycled, and shared by teachers and students alike. (1994, 25)

The Role of Self-Reflection in Socially Responsible Theatre Education

In various ways and times throughout their careers, socially responsible teachers and artists have questioned their own practice in relation to the needs of their students, schools, and communities. Their self-inquiry can be clustered around five questions.

Whose Program Is This?

Who is my program for?

Who is currently being served by this program?

Who is included or excluded from this program?

Whose voice, history, culture, language, aesthetics, and perspectives are heard?

Who is in class, onstage, backstage, "behind the scenes," and in the audience?

Who is the audience?

What Connections Are Made to Students' Lived Experiences?

In what ways is my program responsive to the realities of students' lives?

How am I acknowledging these realities in the work we do?

What Is the Nature of This Learning Community?

How does the way I teach, communicate, and interact with students, staff, parents, and the community acknowledge and address their needs?

How is my program a community for learning, artmaking, and growing in our humanity?

How do I challenge and nurture students while maintaining appropriate professional boundaries?

How Am I Using the Implicit Political Nature of Theatre to Engage Students and the Community?

How am I using theatre as a catalyst for civic dialogue?

How am I inviting multiple-perspective responses to our work?

In what ways does the program reach beyond the school?

Does this work lead to awareness, action, or change?

What Material Do We Study, Develop, and Produce?

> How does the material we use serve this learning community and address their needs?
>
> How does it contribute to, create, perpetuate, or ignore problems?
>
> What is age-appropriate dramatic material?

As questions of this kind arise, some teacher-artists respond by producing plays relevant to their particular students or by developing new classes or projects related to an issue such as bullying, school violence, or gender bias. Middle-school drama teacher Brianna Lindahl chose to address students' concerns about national and world events.

> When [United States troops] went into Afghanistan . . . I created a drama called *The Good War* [based on Studs Turkel's work]. . . . The kids had a little bit of a knowledge of what the Americans were doing and that we had bombed . . . so the activities really brought it to life for them. . . . They knew they were acting, but it touched a really personal [place] . . . brought to life what was going on in the world, and made it relevant to them. (2002b)

Other teachers have restructured their programs to include students from across the school population. Many engage in ongoing self-reflection and use their classes, productions, and interactions with students to heighten awareness, initiate dialogue, and move others in the school and community to action.

The decisions teacher/artists continue to make in terms of socially responsible practice and how extensive or integrated their efforts are within their programs, are based on several factors:

- personal priorities and passions;
- prior educational and practical experience with socially responsible theatre education and/or social activism;
- perception of the purpose of their programs;
- perception of their students' needs;
- time;
- freedom to expand their programs; and
- human and material resources available.

These questions and issues are explored in the remainder of this chapter.

VOICES FROM THE FIELD

Amy Burtaine (2003b) is a teacher–artist who has gone through several cycles of awareness and action in her pursuit of socially responsible theatre practice. For nine months she lived in Rio de Janeiro and studied Theatre of the Oppressed (TO) techniques alongside Augusto Boal and his company. She also applied these techniques with a theatre troupe of youth AIDS educators she formed in Guinea-Bissau, West Africa. She later returned to Brazil to interview Boal and his Jokers (facilitators) about the long-term impact of their work. Amy has taught at the Austin Waldorf School and as a guest artist-teacher at Interlochen Arts Academy. She continues to refine her views and her practice of socially responsible theatre education.

> I believe that there can be no one definition of . . . [socially responsible theatre practice], but that the definition may change depending on the work, the community, and the aims of the work.
>
> All human endeavors are informed by our political, moral, and ethical beliefs. As participating members of society, youth need to be empowered to become socially engaged . . . [meaning] defining and acting from one's beliefs . . . As a theatre educator, it is my goal to bring theatre to students in ways that help them question, critically evaluate, and define themselves and their place in society. At the core of my teaching practice I believe that theatre . . . is the legacy and right of all people, not just those who are "talented," able, or economically privileged. . . . Theatre, as a tool, can become a site for performing democracy. (Burtaine 2003a, b, c)

Theatre and Individual Differences

> Confronting difference is not always comfortable. One response is to ignore the difference and pretend it doesn't matter; another response is to enter into more self-consciously complex relationships with what we perceive as different or foreign.
>
> —SHARON GRADY

In her book *Drama and Diversity*, Sharon Grady (2000) builds awareness about differences of social class, race and ethnicity, gender, sexual orientation, and ability. She provides an indepth examination of each area of difference. She also provides ideas about how drama teachers who work mostly with elementary and middle school children can create dynamic and respectful learning environments inclusive of all students.

In this section, secondary school teacher–artists respond through classroom and production work to the differences Grady identifies, as well as differences of religion, language, and age. Each anecdote highlights how socially responsible theatre teachers are responding to individual differences.

Theatre, Poverty, and Social Class

> The first time I realized we might be poor was when a well-meaning lady at the Southern Baptist church my mother made us go to gave me a bag of clothes. There was an awkward silence as I stared at the bag and then at her. . . . "Thanks," I said with a forced smile, because I knew that was the expected response. . . . On the way home I threw the bag away—and vowed I'd work harder to keep our "situation" our secret.
>
> —SHARON GRADY

Bryar Cougle taught theatre and English at high schools in Virginia and Maryland, and is currently the arts education consultant for the Department of Public Instruction in North Carolina. An articulate advocate for the arts for all children, he reflects on his teaching and production work with students from a rural area in the Southeast and shares strategies he used to build an inclusive, learner-centered program.

> I . . . was teaching in the rural part of Maryland. . . . We were only forty-five minutes down the road from Washington, D.C. Most of [the students] had no clue that that place they saw on television was near them. And many of them were poor, rural people, in many cases still without outdoor plumbing. . . . When you talked about theatre, they weren't even sure, in many cases, necessarily what that really was as opposed to television.
>
> There was a tremendous amount of talent in that community, which had not been tapped. I saw it. I knew it was there. I just had to find it and coax it . . . and I did that. . . . I got kids who, in some cases, couldn't read nor write. So I had to find a way of dealing with that because . . . [they] were really talented kids. But they couldn't read . . . or memorize a script. So I . . . set up a peer mentoring situation where other kids taught them to read a script.

I had . . . what [some] call "the slime" of the school [making theatre] with the valedictorians. . . . I was, I guess, fortunate enough in some cases to find what they needed . . . case by case. . . . It's individual student by individual student.

All of them, I think, come to you. . . . They're attracted to you for something. And for me. . . . I think it was because I had something good going on. My theatre program . . . was visible. . . . It packed a 2,500 seat theatre and . . . [was] one of the central focuses of the school. . . . A lot of kids wanted . . . the visibility. They wanted to do it to prove they could. . . . They wanted to do it for the honor and accolades they got. . . . A lot of them came from . . . broken families, and they saw the theatre as their sort of secondary family. And so their friends became their brothers and sisters, and father and mother in some cases.

I have the typical stories everybody has about individual kids who changed . . . and not so much because of me but because of the opportunities they had as a result of my program. . . . Some of them were saved, from themselves in many cases. . . . One [boy] in particular . . . [who was] . . . functionally illiterate wanted to be in the theatre program. [The] first few shows [he] didn't want to speak, just wanted to hang out and work on crew. But then [he] decided that it was time to . . . [be] in a show. So he went and got some help from one of the other students and read for the show. I cast him. . . . At the time . . . he was overweight, low self-esteem, low achieving. By the time the third year rolled around, his grades had improved, he had lost weight, changed his physical appearance. . . . He didn't go on [to] university and become the rocket scientist. . . . He . . . decided he wanted to go to beautician school. He got a license, started doing hair, and [the] last time I saw him he was making more [money] than I was. But—and he often has said this to me—the reason he was able to do that was because he got enough confidence to say, "Well, let's see what I want to do with my life, and can I do it? Sure I can. I can do anything I want to do." (Cougle 2002)

Theatre, Ability, and Disability

It is often assumed that secondary school theatre is exclusively for the talented, gifted, and able-bodied. However, most socially engaged teachers—including those working in fine arts specialty schools or programs—make it clear that their programs are for all of the students in the school, not just those whose performance abilities or other talents have been developed or are even apparent. In addition, students with disabilities are actively involved in their programs.

Aline Knighton currently teaches theatre at Crockett High School in Austin, Texas. While she was student teaching in Round Rock, Texas with veteran teacher Beryl Knifton, Aline taught a Theatre I class that included five students with a range of physical and cognitive disabilities including cerebral palsy, Down syndrome, and developmental disabilities. Each day these students were excused to return to their classroom a few minutes early to avoid crowded hallways.

On the first day, Beryl took time at the end of class, after [these] students had left, to talk to the remaining students about the privilege they were going to have with these students in their class. She told them to assume that [the students who had left early] were going to be a part of all activities and that they would [all] learn from [each other]. . . . With some very minor adjustments, they participated in all activities except when their aides felt it was not in their best interest.

The thing that was remarkable to me about it had . . . to do with the able-bodied students in that class. Certainly the . . . students [with disabilities] participated and at times moved us to tears with their sensitivity and insight. . . . But in twelve weeks I never saw any student in that class treat their . . . peers with . . . anything but love and respect. . . . No student ever complained about the members of their group, [able-bodied] or not. The students made accommodations so that the assigned work for the . . . students [with disabilities] was within their [range of] abilities.

In one other class we had a young woman who . . . [used] a wheel chair. She was part of a production class and was cast in a role that could accommodate her [physical] challenges. . . . [She] . . . had to have some help onstage since she had limited ability to push her chair for herself. This was easy to accommodate. She also participated in drama club faithfully. (Knighton 2003)

Theatre, Race, and Privilege

> Theatre curricula periodically requires deliberate, focused interrogation, innovation, and reconstruction. . . . As diversity infuses and informs life, we must strive to infuse and expand theatre curricula with diversity.
>
> —Lorenzo Garcia

Tara Affolter teaches theatre and English at East High School in Madison, Wisconsin. Tara's theatre program became her research laboratory as she pursued a graduate degree. In the role of teacher-researcher, she explored how race and white privilege have an impact on students' educational opportunities.

> How are you using the voice that you have in that school? And what are you saying? What are you choosing to say?
>
> —*Tara Affolter*, Teacher

My reason for going back to graduate school in the first place had to do with my frustrations with . . . the way kids of color with sort of harsh lives are pushed aside in schools . . . frustrations with having such a predominantly white theatre program in a multicultural, multiethnic school. . . . [I wanted] to really deconstruct that.

When I started the thesis project, my idea was . . . [to] interview kids of color—the few that were involved in the program already and kids that had been identified or maybe showed up for one audition but then I would never see them again. . . . I realized that the way I was framing the question . . . still put the blame on the kids of color. It was . . . "Why aren't you involved?" rather than . . . "Why would you want to be involved? . . . "What were we doing as the director [and] the kids in the theatre program that could be read as exclusionary?"

I [also] started . . . interviewing [white] . . . kids in the program . . . about what they thought about race, what they thought about . . . the makeup of the program. . . . They really thought racism was something of the past, "back in the day of my grandparents, maybe, but not me." . . . We had to do a lot of processing around that . . . calling kids on some things they may not have seen in a way that wasn't too confrontational. But it made them stop and think. It opened a space for me within the program then to push a little harder. (Affolter 2002)

As Tara's program grows and more students of color are involved, she feels it is essential to look at assumptions about race in terms of casting and character interpretation. In her production of *One Flew Over the Cuckoo's Nest*, for example, Nurse Ratchet was played by an African American student. During rehearsals, Tara and the actor talked about the "invisibility of whiteness that's implicit in the script and what it means for [this] student to play the part" (2002). Tara didn't want the student to think she was being asked to "be" a white woman. Tara encouraged her to see her own identity as an African American woman as part of the character's identity. Tara comments that

> the literature out there is still . . . colorblind white, where it's [as if] anyone can play this part. . . . I . . . refuse to do a show . . . unless . . . you say, "All right, let's look at what is assumed about this character." . . . For me, [what's important is] making the theatre a place where kids can come and . . . see someone like themselves in a role. . . . See . . . it's not just a white kids' thing. It's not just a program for stereotypical theatre kids. . . . We . . . did *The Piano Lesson* by August Wilson [and we] did *Prelude to a Kiss* at the same time because *Piano Lesson* is an all–African American cast, and . . . I don't teach at an all–African American school. . . . I don't want to be exclusionary on any level. (2002)

Tara offers some suggestions for including students from across the school population in the theatre program.

> I think that one of the first things you do is you *ask*. It's as simple as, "Would you like to do this? Would this be something you'd be interested in? . . . Your English teacher said. . . . I saw you in the hallway. . . ." Not being afraid to talk to kids and not just isolating. The other thing that's really important is to not just bring a lone student in unless they're particularly solid. [In my] English classes . . . sometimes [I'll say] just a gentle, "You really ought to try this, and bring so and so with you so that you're not isolated, [so] you don't [feel like you don't] know anybody."
>
> I think you start with the audition process. Offering a couple of different audition times. . . . [I] try to run my auditions like theatre workshops. . . . We might do some kind of physical . . . warm up . . . not too weird, with enough people . . . that [students] realize pretty quickly that no one is looking at them. . . . The key . . . for kids that are new . . . is to not make it too funky or weird or they won't come back. . . . You can't do that right off before kids trust you. . . . I walk around encouraging them. Occasionally we'll do some sort of structured improv activity . . . usually based on what the play is based on. . . . [Have a] big enough group again so nobody feels . . . on the spot. At some point, I do have them read something for me, and I'm as close to them as I can be without sitting onstage with them. . . . Usually just something simple. . . . Just me and the kid and the other director . . . one at a time.
>
> The first two weeks are crucial to making kids feel safe, making them feel like they're a part of something, not just this outsider trying to break in. . . . And this part's tricky. I've got a core group that identifies themselves as The Theatre. They're the theatre clique. . . . [I am] busting up that clique and using the pillar of that clique at

rehearsals to . . . [eliminate the] exclusionary feeling. . . . [I use] double casting . . . [to have a] built in "somebody else" [and] I pair them for double casting . . . building in that kind of time so they can talk about character.

We set it up so they're a built-in community . . . early on. . . . They care for each other. . . . I make a concerted effort to make sure people understand that not everybody has rides—and this isn't along racial lines . . . [I ask] "Who can carpool?"

[After] opening night . . . they come back. "That's the best thing I've ever done!" . . . Slowly [they] bring a friend and bring a friend. I'm not saying I'm where I want to be yet in terms of diversity and its facets . . . but I'm getting there. Socially responsible theatre is [when] you realize that . . . there's a lot of ways that you can reach out, even within the mainstage . . . [model]. [It means] having your students become socially responsible and work toward, in my case, social justice and . . . equity in their own school. . . . The other layer to social responsibility is: What are you saying to the adults, the families, parents, staff that come see this show? . . . . The social responsible piece looks at the bigger picture. . . . "Is it just another show? Or is there more to it than that?" (Affolter 2002)

Theatre, Language, and Culture

They told me the small pastries we made were called "Butterflies." My Mamá called them "Buñuelos." They said my mother was wrong. She said they were called "Buñuelos" in México. They told me it was the "Rio Grande." My Mamá told me it was the "Rio Bravo." They said she was wrong. In México it is the Rio Bravo, she said. They told me Columbus discovered America. My Papá said, how could you discover something when civilizations were already here? They said my father was wrong. They told me that the Aztecs and Incas were savages that ate people. Mis Papas told me that they were astronomers and mathematicians and farmers and writers and warriors, and they took baths, too. They told me my parents were wrong, their stories irrelevant. They told me to stop asking questions. They told me to stop putting the accent on my name. They told me to stop doing my math the way my father showed me. They told me that I should be more like the other boys and girls. They told me that my parents were wrong. They never stopped to think that maybe they were wrong.

—Mónica Byrne-Jiménez

A theatre program seems an ideal place to liberate young people from the boundaries of an English-only curriculum, freeing them to explore ideas beyond the limitations of spoken language. A theatre program is also a place to celebrate the differences of language and culture that walk in the door with each child. As one of my college students queried, "Why do we always start theatre history with the Greeks? Why not start with the Mayans?"

I admire teachers and artists who are multilingual and able to easily interact with students in languages other than English. I also admire those English-speaking teacher-artists who employ innovative strategies for teaching theatre to students who speak the many other languages heard in our schools today. Some theatre teachers devise projects that include a cross section of students who all speak different languages, while others choose to give voice to one or more groups within the school population. Several teacher-directors develop and or produce bilingual plays while others have learned new languages in order to teach their students more effectively.

In the mid-1990s, Roxanne Schroeder-Arce moved to the Texas-Mexico border town of Laredo to begin her first teaching job. There she was cautioned by her colleagues not to learn spanish or speak Spanish in the school.

> A flock of teachers and counselors began to advise me. "Don't let them speak Spanish in your classroom. They'll take advantage of you," and "They get to hear Spanish all day. They should speak English in school. This is America." Despite the advice, I welcomed the Spanish lessons my students offered, and my interest surprised them. Every day, the last fifteen minutes of class, someone would play teacher, and I played student with the rest of the class. . . . I began seeking plays that were culturally relevant to them; we found a couple, we wrote a couple. (2002a)

Roxanne became fluent in Spanish and felt welcomed by Mexican Americans in the community. She wrote several bilingual plays for professional production and later became education director and then artistic director at Teatro Humanidad, a bilingual theatre in Austin, Texas. She writes about the challenges she has faced as a Caucasian woman doing this work.

> I have been careful for quite some time, as a white, female, English-speaking teaching artist in classrooms full of a multitude of cultures, colors, languages, genders, and other orientations. Yet, where does this notion of "being careful" come from, and what does it mean? As an educator, why does consciously discussing my or my students' cultural identity feel like walking on ice? (2002a)

Roxanne reflects about an intensive university class, Diversity Through Drama, that she taught to teachers one summer.

> As I facilitated discussions, I asked [the teachers] to explain and reflect upon their own understanding of and connections to culture. I invited them onto the ice and encouraged them to reflect on icy experiences of their past. (2002a)

During the week, she learned that

> a professional teaching artist in the community . . . [who] was associated with the university had called and complained about the class. . . . This Latino male . . . was outraged that a class on diversity was being taught by a white woman to a classroom of white students . . . I responded . . . that in that case, this man could only teach Latinoism. . . . I shared the gentleman's remark with my students. One responded, "You are not telling us about how you feel being Latino, or black, or Asian; you are helping us to gain skills at empathizing with our students and meeting their needs." We thought about the students in our classrooms . . . how they might share their

cultural experiences and thus "teach culture" to one another. And we voiced our fears, fears that are perpetuated by the feeling that one has to "be" something to understand it, or to teach it. Fears that lead us to believe that we must have lived every experience . . . and speak every language that is spoken in our classrooms in order to teach our students effectively.

I am realizing that the ice I walk on—that we all walk on as "other"—may never melt completely and become firm ground. If the ice were to melt, I could never learn to skate on it, to benefit from the cultural and linguistic challenges I face as an "other." . . . Maybe this is how it should be. (Schroeder-Arce 2002a)

In settings in which many different languages are spoken, teachers effectively use movement, visual images, and music to create works that explore commonalties and differences in language and culture. In other instances, they stage plays that give voice to otherwise silenced children. John Heinemann (2002) and Patsy Koch Johns (2002), who teach together in Lincoln, Nebraska, had an experience that fostered inclusion and sharing of cultures stimulated by a theatre production.

We did *The Rememberer* [by Steven Dietz]. . . . We have about twenty-five Native American [students] at our school, and there's a class called Native American Scholars where [students] get to look at Native American culture. . . . [These students] were really the consultants for the production. They were all involved. Some actually auditioned and were in the show, but many of them . . . talked about . . . [their experience in their nation] . . . even though [where the play is set is] . . . a nation in the Northwest. They had stories to tell, and kids really had a chance to sit down and talk with each other about . . . their culture. . . . These students . . . had never really had a voice in our school.

That play was a very powerful experience not only for the actors onstage . . . [but for the entire school community]. We have twenty-something first languages spoken at Lincoln High, and we have all the flags [of these nations]. Second semester . . . [some Native American students] noticed there were no Native American nation flags there. . . . Then they did this assembly—a whole ceremony—in front of the school. They blessed [their nations'] flags . . . [and] spoke about their nations. . . . They never could have done that without the experience of having *The Rememberer* on that stage first semester. . . . Then second semester they're up there telling their own . . . stories. (Heinemann 2002)

Theatre and Gender

There was a child went forth every day
And the first object he looked upon, that object he became
And that object became part of him for a day or a certain part of the day,
Or for many years or stretching cycles of years.
—WALT WHITMAN

I think that probably just by being a woman who teaches stagecraft I'm . . . breaking down a lot of stereotypes. . . . They walk in the door, and they're like "Uh, you're our stagecraft teacher?" [I] always . . . wear a skirt the day that I teach the saws . . . just to help remind them that "You know what, girls can do this too." I think it's a way of teaching without ever having to say a word.

—Valerie Roberts Labonski, Teacher

Jennifer Chapman, a theatre artist and teacher from Madison, Wisconsin, has investigated the development of girls' role identification as females. She has questioned how the characters we ask adolescent girls to play onstage might impact their gender development (2002). Jennifer wrote an article about a high school production of *Damn Yankees* that she saw. Her ideas have particular relevance to a discussion of socially responsible theatre education.

From behind the curtain came the actress: a fifteen or sixteen year-old girl dressed in a sequined, red dress which generously reveals her voluptuous figure. She paraded the stage in heels and stockings, belting her song: "Whatever Lola wants . . . Lola gets," her hips signaling the downbeats to the music. Gradually she moved off the stage and into the house, interacting with the audience as she sang, making playful eye contact with willing male observers, and cooing to the supportive laughter and applause that met her. . . .

I felt uncomfortable, embarrassed, and generally ill at ease at the sight of a "pompom girl" (as stated in her bio) performing a character who promised the audience sexual pleasures if they could give her what she wanted. Throughout her song, "Lola" is explaining to a weak male soul that he will not be able to defend himself against her sexual prowess. She breaks away from the action on stage and continues her story/song to the audience, enticing them with her sexual power. Her job is to collect souls for her willful keeper/protector/employer, the devil. Their interactions spark laughter throughout the play, but it occurred to me that Lola's subservient position was demeaning and might not seem so funny if the characters were more realistic.

I left the theatre confused by my negative reaction to a scene that everyone else in the audience appeared to enjoy. I was also concerned that my reaction was somehow related to this teenage actor's recognition of her sexual self. Shouldn't teenagers be allowed to express themselves as sexual beings who have the ability, experience, and maturity to understand those experiences? Yes, definitely. But what about when that means objectifying a woman's body and portraying it as a sexual vehicle for power and control? And what does it mean that the young woman is heartily applauded for playing this character?

My experience at *Damn Yankees* caused me to reflect on the importance of providing adolescent girls with roles and entire plays that challenge traditional constructions of female gender, express some element of their own life experiences, and provide a vehicle for self-reflection and growth. . . . If theatre is to provide an opportunity for a creative exploration of self, then we must be considerate of the unique "selves" of adolescent performers; I don't think this has to be contradictory to enjoying the process of creating a play. The challenge for theatre practitioners, teachers, and scholars is to expand the repertoire of plays for high school students to include more pieces that can achieve both. (Chapman 2000)

Do onstage experiences inform students' offstage perceptions of themselves and others? What elements in a script should teacher-directors consider when selecting plays to produce with adolescents? Examination of gender roles and gender bias in a secondary school program is an area ripe for further consideration by teacher-artists as well as researchers (Chapman 2002).

There have been many theatre projects in recent years, prompted by the work of Pipher, Orenstein, and others, that have examined multiple views of what it means to be female in our country. A number of teachers and artists have undertaken projects around this theme. (A sample lesson from such a project is included in Chapter 5 on page 151.) Others strive to make their theatre classrooms gender fair (Bishop 1992; Metz and McNally 2001). As Bishop says, "Gender-fair education refers to curriculum and teaching methods that adequately support and meet the needs of both girls and boys" (1992, 7). There have been research

Figure 3–1 **Both girls and boys assume leadership roles in a gender fair theatre program.**

studies, articles, and books written about boys' gender development (Garbarino 1999; Kindlon and Thompson 2000; Pollack 1998, 2000). Interestingly, I found no teacher-artists who have developed performances or classroom work exploring the paths from boyhood to manhood.

Theatre and Sexual Orientation

Gender identification in a theatre program is related in some instances to recognition of differences in sexual orientation. I taught drama to teachers at a theatre institute one summer with Jason Ewing, a drama teacher from Evanston, Illinois. Jason was using *From the Notebooks of Melanin Sun*[1] to demonstrate how a book could be used as a springboard into drama for older elementary and middle school students. Two teachers borrowed and read the whole book, which later in the text includes the heterosexual awakening of the young protagonist against the backdrop of his discovery of his mother's homosexuality. The teachers were taken aback by the material and concerned how parents and administrators would respond. While Jason had no intention of using the whole book in the classroom, he acknowledged that some students might be interested in reading it since his drama work with the story leaves off early in the book just before the mother brings a visitor home for her son to meet. Jason describes *Melanin Sun* and the way he handles sensitive material in the classroom.

> I use the piece in such a way . . . that I . . . give them just a little bit of dramatic information and then let them make choices. . . . I don't do the literature in a linear fashion. . . . At first it's just getting to know who these characters are and really doing a character study. . . . What is it like to live in Brooklyn in the summer on the third floor in Hell's Kitchen? And what is it like to live in a community where you hear all these different languages and you see kids bouncing up and down [in the street] on box springs? . . . What is it like to be a kid who doesn't feel comfortable with all the other kids? . . . It's really interesting to me to see what comes from those dramas.
>
> We hear the history of how Mom got this family of two into this neighborhood. And it brings up issues of the father who's not there, and how do you define father, and should people feel sorry for kids who don't have fathers 'cause they don't know any different? So, it brings up a lot of good issues that fifth graders can talk about.
>
> In . . . [the] part of the story [where] Melanin's mother tells Melanin that she's bringing someone home for dinner . . . and she wants Melanin to be there, he says, "Wait a minute, you're not getting married are you?" So she's . . . concerned that his paradigm is going to have to be shifted. So what's interesting to me is to see what scenes they come up with. I call it the "Guess who's coming to dinner" scene. (Ewing 2002)

Jason goes on to discuss why and how he chooses to use controversial material in the classroom.

> I've been really careful . . . when I pick literature [for drama work]. I make sure that either the literature has won an award, has been reviewed by the American Library

Association, [or] is a current book [in a library] somewhere in town, so that it does not appear that I am . . . forcing beliefs or forcing cultural mores onto students . . . I'm really careful in how we talk about this. But you know, we have [local, state, and national] standards that talk about current events. And so, thankfully, because we have a free media, that kind of leaves the door open for just about anything.

After September 11th, we did a lot of talking about stereotypes, a lot of talking about why is it that cultures are perceived in certain ways. . . . I brought in some Muslim literature. I brought in some literature from Africa that was not Judeo-Christian in its beliefs. I brought in books about Animism. And we looked at them and said, "Wait a minute. How does this change our beliefs?" And we also talked about the importance of education. I said, "You know who gets to be educated in Afghanistan?" So . . . you can bring up current events. And the fifth-grade teachers do current events in their classrooms, which gives me the entranceway to do things with that in the drama classroom. (Ewing 2002)

Jerry Smith teaches theatre at Salem High School in LaGrange, Georgia. He feels sexual orientation will naturally emerge as a topic in a theatre program.

With our kids . . . one of the things we try to do is deal with gay issues because we certainly have gay students in the building . . . and in the department. I think what theatre allows us to do is . . . work through, in a conscious setting, things that we would only subconsciously think about. Because in the guise of an improv, you can say some of those things that you might think but you sure would not say standing in the middle of a commons area. Or you might get that interesting look on your face when someone says something about someone gay. And there is then the opportunity to [discuss] that. (Smith 2002)

Nancy Wilkinson's theatre students became socially engaged in response to incidents of sexual harassment in her school.

This year [there were] . . . problems for some students [who] are gay. . . . One boy was beaten up at a dance because he brought a guy. Another boy had his car . . . vandalized because he's gay. . . . So when we did *What Is Your Dream* . . . for Martin Luther King [Day], we incorporated the whole gay issue . . . not just . . . a dream for being ethical and having dignity and inclusiveness for all races and religions, [but also] for sexual orientation. Now that would not have been a focus five, ten years ago when I was teaching theatre, but it is right now, at least . . . this year. So we dealt with it through that piece. (Wilkinson 2002)

Patsy Koch Johns, who teaches with John Heinemann in Lincoln, Nebraska, explored issues related to sexual orientation when she directed *The Laramie Project*. That production, like *The Rememberer*, had a profound impact on both faculty and students.

There is not a day that goes by that I do not remember the story of Mathew Shepard and *The Laramie Project*. A student enters my room [who] . . . has to tell me a story that relates to the experience they had while working on the show. I encounter situations that require the courage to stand up and repeat what I learned—that violence begins small—with the words we choose to say to each other every day. Directing, acting, analyzing, studying *The Laramie Project* altered many lives . . . I believe, for the better. It gave us all a keen awareness of our own personal power to change the world with our small everyday actions. That power can be used to do good or to do evil. (Johns 2003)

There are other aspects of sexual orientation to be considered. For a majority of teachers, public knowledge of *their* sexual orientation is not an issue affecting their practice. For others, especially those who are gay, lesbian, or transgendered, knowledge of their sexual orientation can present challenges including harassment, rumors, isolation, ridicule, and inappropriate or unwanted sexual advances. Jennifer Chapman (2002) talked about the importance of dialogue surrounding this issue. She and a fellow graduate student at the University of Wisconsin were commissioned to devise and present a performance ethnography piece entitled *Wearing the Secret Out* (Chapman, Sykes, and Swedberg 2003). The performance they were commissioned to develop is a moving, stylized dramatization of excerpts from interviews with gay, lesbian, and bisexual physical education teachers. The piece was shown at professional associations and to the intended audience, preservice teachers, which stimulated dialogue about problems teachers can face in their interactions with colleagues, parents, and students. As Jennifer noted, conversations among peer teachers and candid discussion of concerns prior to entering the teaching force can help prepare teachers for their interactions with coteachers, staff, students, and parents. Dialogue enables everyone to thrive in a safe and respectful work environment.

Theatre, Religion, and Spirituality

> There is a principle which is a bar against all information, which is proof against all arguments and which cannot fail to keep a man in everlasting ignorance—that principle is contempt prior to investigation.
>
> —HERBERT SPENCER

Hate crimes and religious intolerance, unfortunately, are not things of the past in this country. I know of incidents where children are subtly excluded from social gatherings when their friends' parents learn they aren't the "right" religion. Recently, one of my students talked to me about his experiences with religious discrimination when he was in high school. Some people in his community learned that his mom identified herself as a pagan. They reacted with violence, setting a fire on the walk to the student's home and burning hateful messages in his front yard. My student was harassed on the way to school and at school. These behaviors, and the attitudes leading to them, beg for interrogation, discussion, and action.

In some academic settings there is a palpable silence around issues of religion and spirituality due, perhaps, to concerns about separation of church and state. This silence may be confusing or disconcerting to young people for whom their faith or their family's faith is a vital part of their identity. Assumptions about organized religion in general, stereotypes about specific faiths, confusion between spirituality and religion, and legal questions can leave educators unsure how to respond to issues that might come up in school. Young people, "religious" or not, can become vulnerable to criticism and misinformed about students or faculty with whom they must work closely. Educators, however, can make incidents of prejudice or religious discrimination opportunities for inquiry, tolerance, and expanded appreciation. Teachers can address biases and misinformation in the area of religion and faith like they do in the areas of difference discussed earlier.

Deb Alexander had occasion to interrupt some misconceptions about Judaism while teaching her middle school students. They were discussing *The Diary of Anne Frank* and Deb was talking with her students about anti-Semitism during the Nazi era.

> I chose to tell them the stories that my grandparents had told me about surviving the Holocaust. I also used several visuals to tell Anne Frank's story. Halfway through my presentation, one of my students asked me, "Are we all Jews?" At first I thought he was being a smart aleck, but then I realized that he had no idea what a "Jew" was. It turned out only five members of the class knew that Judaism was a religion. I needed to back up and explain Judaism. Now, I was in very sticky territory because I didn't want to be teaching a religion lesson. Students asked, "What does a Jew look like?" "How can you tell if you're Jewish?" and "Hitler looks like a Jew." This actually led into an entirely new lesson, which proved to be an excellent experience for both the students and myself. We ended up tying the discussion into the Martin Luther King holiday and the oppression of African Americans in the United States. (Alexander 1999)

Holly Stanfield is a teacher and a performing artist from Kenosha, Wisconsin. She produces provocative theatre pieces and musicals with students. Two of her recent shows touched on the subjects of prayer, religion, race, and other areas of difference. She staged Mark Twain's "The War Prayer," written originally for choir, symphony, and soloist. The same year they also did *Parade*, a musical set in Atlanta and based on the 1912–1913 Leo Frank case. Holly describes *Parade* and why she chose to produce it.

> A Jewish man . . . [is] . . . railroaded and accused for a young girl's rape and murder. Eventually he's lynched. . . . The show approaches race issues, black/white, [and] Judeo/Christian issues, North/South issues, male/female prejudice issues. It goes through the whole gamut of issues that we faced at that point in our history. . . . [It gave] us . . . an opportunity to discuss some of those things in class and let the kids think. . . . And I think they're old enough to think. . . . I think they want to. Some of them don't. Some are going to be really uncomfortable, but this is an elective. . . . If they want to come and meet us at this level, and they're ready for that discussion, then they'll come. (Stanfield 2002)

These are incredibly powerful and empowering moments that happen [unexpectedly] in classes. If I don't throw whatever we're doing out the window and address them, I think [I'm] being irresponsible . . . . My charge is to educate. That's what [I'm] supposed to be doing.
—*Rebecca Jallings*, Teacher

Figure 3–2 *Socially responsible theatre education includes producing plays with complex, controversial themes relevant to students' lives. (A scene from* Parade *directed by Holly Stanfield)*

Theatre and Age-Appropriate Practice

[Students] understand that a high school is a certain kind of an audience. [In improvs] I don't want to hear about drugs. I don't want to hear about sex. . . . This is the way we need to do things because [they're] still kids.

—HOLLY STANFIELD, TEACHER

Some teacher-artists wrestle with balance when it comes to socially responsible practice. A number have decided that emphasis on current events or social issues should not be the *primary* focus of their programs. This perspective is based on a desire to protect the social and mental well-being of students or to focus primarily on theatre study and theatre making. Fursey Gotuaco articulates the challenge of trying to strike a balance.

> Sometimes . . . something happens in the real world, and I'll discuss it, pull it in . . . do something with it and process that. And then there's another half [of me] that says, "You know, this must be the one place where they get to get away from all that.". . . I think there's a balance to be had. I think that theatre is the best tool in the building to make them come to grips with their emotions and the realities of the world . . . but . . . theatre is also probably the best tool in the building to give them an escape from the pressures that they feel in the world. (2002)

Others, like David O'Fallon, former director of the Perpich Center for the Arts in St. Paul, feel that we can't be naive about who is sitting in our classrooms.

> They're caring for siblings. They're working at Burger King. . . . They're doing the bagging at a supermarket. They're involved in very heavy family issues . . . sometimes with a lot of responsibility for home life. And then they come to school, and we treat them like they're six-year-olds rather than working with them to enforce their sense of responsibility and growth. . . . At the Perpich Center . . . we tried to . . . give kids more choices and responsibility and let them live with the consequences of some of their choices. (2002)

Until I started writing this book, I hadn't thought about ageism as having anything to do with young people. Yet, as I visit schools and observe and interact with teachers, artists, and young people, I grow more convinced that there are important age-related questions to consider. What is age-appropriate in a secondary school theatre program? What is too much, not enough, or the right combination of exposure to contemporary societal issues for children eleven to nineteen years old? What is the balance between what is age-appropriate, what is socially responsible, and what is curricularly relevant? In centuries past, thirteen-year-olds were fighting wars and having babies. For many of our children, this is still the truth of their life today. They are facing gang warfare daily in their neighborhoods and the consequences of early sexual activity in their own lives and the lives of their families and friends. While some American children are able to grow from childhood to adulthood under the nurturing and attentive care of mature, responsible adults, we can't assume this is true for all of our students. How do we acknowledge, address, and accommodate this truth in our theatre programs?

Teachers and artists are working to find answers to these questions in part by addressing difference in their classrooms and productions. In the long run, however, questions of this magnitude will be answered not by theories, formulas, or examples in a book, but, as Bryar Cougle suggests, "individual student by individual student" (2002).

It is our nation's shame that we continue to neglect our children's emotional lives and murder their dreams. I hope and pray that one day soon society will accept the truth that artistic process needs to become an integral part of every human being's daily life, especially our young.
—Robert Alexander

Patsy Koch Johns eloquently summarizes the need for socially responsible theatre education programs.

> We're all in our own little worlds. And that's what theatre is about, taking you into somebody else's world and making you see the world through their eyes. Once we get in our little house and we make our little breakfast and dinner and we get in our little cars and go to work . . . , it's like Mr. Magoo—we become nearsighted, and if everything is all right in our little world, then it must be all right in the rest of the world as well. Theatre takes us out of our world into other worlds. I think it gives us an opportunity to mind-travel, and then . . . to become better human beings, more responsible human beings because we're responsible, not just to our little microcosm but to the whole entire world. . . . We're educating young people to be responsible to the world . . . not just *their* world. (Johns 2002)

Making Connections to Students' Lived Experiences

> The program at Lexington High School is structured so that we always take it back to the kids' lives. For example, if we're doing a piece on status . . . we always look at status in their lives. What that does is makes the process circular for the kids so that they understand they're not just looking at something on the stage or characters or something in the movies. They're actually looking at things that play out in their lives.
> —Sandra DiMartino, Teacher

The first time I walked into a theatre was the first time I was wonderful at something.

—Patsy Koch Johns, Teacher

Another aspect of socially responsible theatre education is how students relate to the material studied and produced. Not only do teachers and directors draw from and connect curriculum to relevant aspects of students' lives, they consciously select topics and material to interrupt assumptions and to cause a shift in students' understanding of themselves and others. While some teachers make clear that everything they do doesn't relate directly to students' lives, they emphasize that there are natural and relevant connections to be found in most lessons and productions. For example, students working on *Romeo and Juliet* may not be considering suicide or facing gang violence, but they can identify with defying or being thwarted by authority figures or being part of a group that is either privileged or excluded from certain activities. Links like these can open discussion and engage students in theatre making and reflective learning.

As many teachers have learned, merely working with plays that might somehow relate to students' lives doesn't automatically result in a shift in understanding or a change in behavior. We must deliberately help students find connections —a transfer of insight—between what happens onstage and what happens in the world. This transfer is a goal of both classroom work and formal theatre projects and must be facilitated by a skilled teacher-director.

We all have seen lives change as students participate in our programs. One can't help but wonder, however, how we identify transfer or transformation resulting from classroom and production work, especially when one of our goals is a shift in students' understanding of themselves, their fellow humans, and their world. Assessment and evaluation models, even portfolios, document fairly short periods of time and often don't capture the transfer of new understandings to lived experiences beyond the classroom or school. If transformations happen out of our line of vision—sometimes long after students have left our classrooms and rehearsal halls—how can we determine what has transferred and so refine our curriculum and artistic interactions? JoBeth Gonzalez and I have had lengthy conversations about transfer and the resultant joys and disappointments (Gonzalez 2002b). In her article investigating transfer and transformation, she writes about what many of us may have felt in our hearts.

> In my darkest moments, I regretfully sigh and wonder if any play has the power to truly influence teens to change their lifestyles or attitudes . . . I know that adolescents are egocentric and they learn to situate themselves in society by taking risks to discover boundaries. I know I should accept the discontinuities, and accept the impossibilities of full understanding. I know I should expect the impact of our work with students to be inconsistent, so I must come to terms with contradiction. I should be happy for moments of connectedness. (Gonzalez 2002a, 19)

Some teachers are concerned about connectedness and what some may call "failed transfer." This is when students separate the ideas explored in the play or lesson from their lives, those frustrating moments when, for instance, after a thought-provoking rehearsal related to gender bias, a student then speaks rudely and disparaging about girls (or boys) in the parking lot with friends. JoBeth calls these "misconnects" or "breakdowns" rather than "failed transfers" and feels they are to be embraced as part of democratic, learner-centered practice. "The particular plays that we select for our students to explore through production give students the opportunity to examine their own lives, but students must choose to make the effort" (2002a, 20). JoBeth concludes,

> As I and other high school theatre teachers coach students to discover meaning in the plays they participate in, we will find the challenge to guide students no less difficult, but we might accept those resistances as part of the process of teaching. . . . We welcome "breakdowns" for the fresh insights they may bring to our understanding of our students, to our curriculum, and to ourselves. (2002a, 19, 21)

We also can't fairly determine impact from a few students who haven't chosen to transfer to their lives ideas from a class or production or have done so selectively. Assumptions about impact, positive or negative, shouldn't distort our work or serve as excuses for "business as usual" or for an unwillingness to raise difficult questions with students and audiences.

Building a Safe Learning Community

We build a community where kids can grow in their humanness.
—Jerri Castlebury, Teacher

One overarching aspect of socially responsible theatre education is that sense of belonging, of being noticed and valued, that students can feel in a theatre program. As theatre teachers, we are in a position to notice, respond to, and influence how our students see themselves, their peers, and the world in which they live. Being willing to accept this influential role with maturity and sensitivity is best practice.

It is impossible to calculate the impact one teacher can have on a student's life. I recently read an account of a young woman who overcame depression and isolation because a teacher took an active interest in a book she was reading (Markowitz 2003). How do teacher-artists carry principles of learner-centered instruction and socially responsible practice into their whole theatre program and the school community?

Jerry Smith, who teaches in Georgia, notes that "teachers spend more time with kids . . . than parents do." His program operates as a community and includes parents in appropriate ways.

Figure 3–3 *A theatre program can be a safe place for students to talk, be heard, and feel appreciated.*

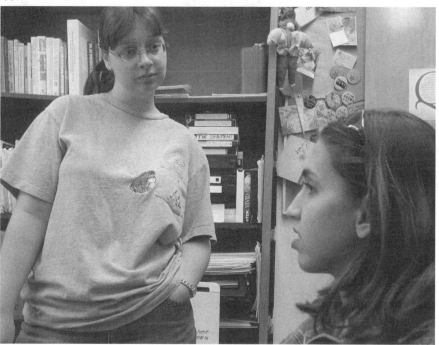

[It is important] . . . for parents to understand how their kids are working their hands off. . . . I [also] think our students learn a tremendous amount from the fact that parents are here. They're welcome to be here. They're not forced to be here. . . . Our parents are in and out of rehearsals. They feed us the week and a half before a show. . . . I would not have a program, it would not be educationally sound, if that part of the community wasn't involved.

I believe that without parents involved, you don't have the full conversation. . . . Sometimes, that's a negative conversation, which is fine. . . . I love it when a parent wants to challenge. . . . Then there can be a dialogue. . . . We, as a school community, we, as a theatre community, have to be open to the dialogue, not be afraid of it, but be open to it. (Smith, J. 2002)

Figure 3–4 *A scene from Peoples Light and Theatre production of the* **Little Prince.**

VOICES FROM THE FIELD

For Holly Stanfield, creating safe and respectful community and long-term commitments to students is important.

> The rule . . . [is]: It has to be safe. That's it. Which means . . . when you get into the improv . . . some of the scenes [might become hurtful]. . . . Kids know when you're laughing 'cause it's funny or when you're laughing to be mean. . . . So, if you're laughing to be mean, you can drop the class now. That means you just aren't mature enough to do this yet. You can come back again. I'll love you either way. We'll talk, and your parents and I will talk, but you can't do that here. . . . If kids are going to grow in a community, that's just not possible. And it's kind of a collective sigh of relief when they really realize that [this] class is going to run that way. And they all make the decision, "OK, I know I can't do that, so I won't." (Stanfield 2002)

Creating a Home Within the Program

> *As a high school freshman, I dressed differently than many of my classmates and faced ridicule for it. I was withdrawn from much of the . . . school until I joined the . . . theatre department at the end of the year. . . . I was quickly accepted into a group of friends that actually praised me for my need for individuality. What was even better was that this department was molded [by] some of the coolest teachers I have ever met. Their constructive criticism allowed me to open up and help add to the department. . . . I hope one day to teach in a public school in the same way my high school mentors have.*
>
> —Ben Gooding, Preservice Teacher

We all have treasured stories from students about the impact our theatre programs have had on students' lives. Both teachers and students attribute much of this impact to the fact that their theatre programs are safe havens for students in socially, emotionally, or physically hostile school environments. Students speak of their secondary school theatre program as a "community," "home," "family," and "place where I feel I belong." The programs they are speaking about are open to all students in the school, especially those who feel they don't fit in anywhere else.

Teachers in these programs make apparent to students that *what* they teach and produce, and *how* they teach and produce, directly relates to the students' interests and concerns. They are consistent in encouraging inquiry and ownership in their classrooms, in rehearsals, and in other interactions with students. The ongoing dialogue and assessment that characterizes their learner-centered, socially responsible classrooms enlivens their entire theatre programs.

Rebecca Jallings highlights the gap a theatre program can fill in students' school experience.

> One of the things the kids say in their final exams a lot is . . . "This is the only class . . . I've ever had where I learned everybody's name." . . . A retired teacher . . . who I really respect said that what happens in a classroom between the kids in the class and the teacher . . . that community of people, is mystical and sacred . . . I think she's right. On a good day it's mystical and sacred. You can't leave out pieces of it. And you can't expect people to have a mystical and spiritual and sacred experience in a group of people whose names they don't even know. What the hell is that? (2002)

VOICES FROM THE FIELD

Justine Johnson was active in her theatre program as a high school student. She reflects about the impact of that experience on her as a student, an adult, and as a parent of a high school student.

> I tried out for my first play the fall of my first year . . . and I actually got a part. It wasn't a very big part, I didn't even have lines, but as I heard many times "there are no small parts, only small actors." After that I was hooked . . . I worked on every production during my high school years.
>
> My teacher at the time played a big part in my experiences. . . . She also spent quite a bit of time with us [at rehearsals after] school. We knew she cared about us . . . . We knew she was our instructor, that she had authority over us as any other teacher would, but she didn't lord it over us; she treated us like the adults we were becoming. . . . As we became [more] independent . . . from our homes . . . , we were safe in our drama family. We were able to be individuals and learn how to be self-sufficient participants in a social situation that was safe. We learned responsibility as we each had tasks that were integral to the production, however small in themselves, still a part of the whole.
>
> Some of my best friends in high school were those I met during drama. When you spend so much time with people, they become like family. . . . There are some I still keep in touch with, even after twenty-plus years. I even correspond with my [teacher].
>
> I believe my experience in drama in high school helped me become the person I am today. It was a positive learning experience that afforded . . . good practice for the "real" world. . . . Now I have a teenager in high school [who] is delving into the drama department . . . I hope he . . . can gain as much as I did. (Johnson 2003)

Building Relationships Within the Program

> Lara was very shy, very reserved, as a ninth grader. She was taller than most all of her classmates, including the boys. . . . [She] didn't carry herself with any air of confidence. . . . She had rounded shoulders and her arms were crossed most of the time, closing herself off to others around her. When she entered the theatre department, she didn't seem to fit in . . . until . . . a senior [student] costumer in the department extended her hand to include Lara on her costume crew. . . . We started to see changes take place in Lara. Little by little, pieces of Lara's shell started to crack. . . . Lara is [now] a senior at Carnegie Mellon University . . . [and her] costume designs . . . will be seen on the Carnegie Mellon stage [this year]. . . . There is a place for everyone in theatre.
> —Carlen Gilseth, Teacher

How do teachers and students build a safe place within schools? As teacher-artists, many of our interactions with students occur outside of our classrooms or rehearsals during crew calls, drama club or Thespian events, fundraisers, or informal gatherings. In our informal interactions with students, we can establish a culture that makes clear to students that our program is inclusive or exclusive. We can create a community that either invites or discourages authentic participation by all students.

Teachers invent ways to make their theatre programs inviting places of discovery and celebration: doors are open when work is going on; social needs of the adolescents are addressed through celebrations of accomplishments, cleanup days, field trips, welcome-back and end-of-year festivities; current and prospective members of the program are included; and students serve as formal or informal ambassadors to students new to the department.

Opportunities to be of service in the school and community allow teenagers to move beyond themselves while still being anchored in the safe harbor of a community that values theatre, artmaking, and their individual contributions. All of these interactions among and between students and teacher-directors are characterized by principles of best practice. An inclusive, learner-centered culture is at the foundation of these programs.

Many teachers are also active in the life of their schools. Laurel Serleth (2002) used theatre to build community within her urban Evanston, Illinois, school. Working with the fifth grade drama club, she devised a piece based on the dreams of all those in the building. Students collected dreams from other students, the custodians, teachers, and administrators. The night dreams and nightmares of the school population as well as their daydreams, hopes, and desires were staged in a bilingual, eclectic performance for the whole school.

In Fursey Gotuaco's school, the principal thinks of him and the theatre program almost as an extension of the administration. The principal turns to Fursey (2002) and coteacher Jenny Lutringer (2002b) for advice and solutions to issues in the larger school community. Brianna Lindahl (2002b) brings her drama skills into service for her school as well. She has developed a process drama and uses Boal's (1985) Forum Theatre techniques in workshops and programs with faculty and staff.

Sandy DiMartino found a way to respond to an administrator's concerns while unifying students and teachers at her high school in Lexington, Massachusetts.

> This year we held a Renaissance Fair. . . . Our goal was to have more of the adults [teachers and staff] involved. . . . We had adults singing and performing and reading tarot cards. . . . It brought kids and adults together in a way they wouldn't normally be brought together. . . . One of my agendas . . . was to make . . . connections so the adults had . . . an understanding of the types of students who were working with us and also of the work involved. . . . Also, the principal has spoken with me about ways in which to . . . help connect the [school] community more because the adults in our school are all . . . [physically] separated from each other. . . . One of the other agendas was just to help the adults see each other and connect. . . . The feedback was overwhelmingly positive. (2003)

Creating an environment in which students can safely explore ideas and challenges that will help them grow into healthy adults is an admirable goal. It can also serve a larger social purpose by allowing young people to practice healthy interactions with peers and adults and to imagine life beyond high school.

Steve Bogart teaches with Sandy DiMartino at Lexington High School. In his Drama of Social Issues class, students devise and perform two original pieces for the school during the semester. In their improvisation classes, he and Sandy challenge students to be socially engaged and to look at their actions from multiple perspectives. In one lesson, for example, they invite students to journal about and then improvise a conflict they had with an authority figure. In this paired improv, students play the authority figure and coach the actor playing them. As a result, they have seen students change their perspective about the conflict and initiate new relationships with adults. (This "Conflict with Authority" lesson is included on pages 91–93.)

Others see theatre programs serving an intervention function, redirecting students into productive activity. In her 1999 essay responding to the shootings at Columbine High School, Holly Giffin discusses how theatre programs can help our young people imagine multiple solutions to the dramas they live out each day at school. Betty Staley furthers this idea by stating that "Through drama, adolescents are able to try out roles, experiment with anger, confrontation, sensitivity, compassion and sacrifice, and to vicariously experience what happens to people in different life situations (1988, 14–15). It is far too speculative to consider if tragic events have been avoided because someone got involved with or stayed active in a secondary school theatre program, but it does give educators hope for more research in this area when we see young people avoid involvement in gangs or abstain from drugs, alcohol, or other dangerous behaviors because they are in a theatre program where they feel "at home."

Personal Interactions with Students

> Education as the practice of freedom—as opposed to education as the practice of domination—denies that man is abstract, isolated, independent, and unattached to the world; it also denies that the world exists as a reality apart from people.
>
> —Paulo Freire

> True personal freedom and self-expression can flower only in an atmosphere where attitudes permit equality between student and teacher and the dependencies of teacher for student and student for teacher are done away with. The problems within the subject matter will teach both of them.
>
> —Viola Spolin

I don't care whether it's math class or phys. ed., you don't pass up a chance to talk about issues of ethics and morals and empathy . . . I'm a teacher. Theatre happens to be my discipline; but I'm a teacher. That's what I do.

—Rebecca Jallings, Teacher

Many teachers feel that the very nature of our work—the exploration of controversial, amusing, or provocative issues, the investigation of intense emotions, the dynamics of human interactions within the company and the school, and the sheer number of hours spent with young people—demands that teachers set personal boundaries and establish shared understandings of protocol and procedures. Many teachers have handbooks that spell out everything from the philosophy of the program to audition procedures, from shop rules to rules for field trips, and rules for appropriate student-student and teacher-student interactions.

Bryar Cougle comments about why setting personal boundaries is important.

> I think . . . part of the reason that teachers experience a lot of burnout [is] because . . . you get very close to kids. If you work closely with students, both instructionally and after school—which also is instructional but on a more personal level—you can't avoid [it] . . . because kids bring their stuff to you, and you end up being a part of that whether you volunteered for it or not. So the work becomes . . . professional work that you have to deal [with] on a very emotional level with kids and with your own self sometimes. . . . Aside from the physical work of being a drama teacher, and the mental work of being a drama teacher, and all the things you have to attend to just to teach every day and keep an after-school program going . . . then you heap on top of that dealing with individual kids who need something from you or need something from . . . the environment you have created . . . that's hard. That's a very hard job. It's a balancing act to keep it all going and not step on any toes, not to get in any trouble. (2002)

There are teachers who *have* gotten into trouble because they haven't created a safe, respectful environment for students. I know of a teacher who swears at students and refers to them, to their faces, as "a—holes" and "losers." I am told he keeps his job because he's a great director. We all have heard stories of teachers who actively socialize with students, share intimate details of their personal lives, supply them with alcohol, get mired in the personal minutiae of their lives, or who leave them unsupervised, working alone on ladders or with power tools. Many new and veteran teachers also have confused the love students feel for the theatre with love for them.

So where do we draw the line between being a compassionate, caring adult professional, and a friend, confidante, lay therapist, or buddy? Despite signs and protests of maturity, secondary-school students are still children who need our protection, guidance, and sound professional judgement. A number of teachers counsel that drawing boundaries for students shows respect for them. They advise:

- Never confuse your job with yourself. Kids love the work which is different from you in the work.

- Recognize the power you wield and use it with benevolence toward all. Favoritism is more about your ego than their learning.

- If students start to disclose information to you that puts them or others at risk, let them know that you, by law, will have to share this information with a counselor or other appropriate person. Offer to go with them to the counselor's office.

- Don't share your own secrets or personal information with students unless you want it shared with others. Not only will students tell others what you say and do, they will embellish and distort the truth, intentionally or not.

- Learn your district's policies and your school's procedures for crisis management. Work with administrators, parents, teachers, and students to amend policies and procedures so that they address unique circumstances that may arise in your program.

- Never be alone with a student in a room with the door closed.

- Take the work seriously. Don't ever take yourself too seriously.

- Make a life for yourself outside of school. It will make you a better teacher.

Theatre as a Catalyst for Dialogue: Community Connections

We need to bring the neighbor back to the hood.

—Grace Lee Boggs

A teacher at the high school nearest to the World Trade Center . . . gathered the writing of the students who witnessed history firsthand. Their school was used as a law enforcement command post, and many of the students, unable to return to their school, turned to art, theater, and photography and writing to express their emotions. [They wrote] monologues, based on interviews with students, faculty and staff, [and] put a hopeful perspective on a monumental tragedy, demonstrating the remarkable spirit of our nation's children.

—Jeanette Larson

The examples in this book clearly depict theatre programs where classroom and production projects serve as catalysts for dialogue, community building, and new connections. Many teacher-artists work to connect the school with the larger community and the community with the school. A number have devised pieces and offer productions in community venues and other area schools.

Tory Peterson offers one example of this outreach. He teaches in St. Paul where he uses his curriculum to link students to issues in other Minnesota communities. Students conduct interviews with community members and then create original theatre pieces based on their research. He describes one project in particular:

> My students are reading *Main Street* by Sinclair Lewis this summer. . . . When we meet in the fall, [we'll] talk about . . . the issues raised . . . then I will turn my students loose in small-town Minnesota—whichever small town they choose to go to—to look at economics, labor, cultural diversity . . . [and topics] in Lewis's play [like] provincialism, institutionalism—so it's all . . . connected. (Peterson, T. 2002)

Examples of community and school connections are further explored in Chapter 5.

Choosing Socially Responsible Material to Teach and Produce

Socially responsible theatre education means that the material produced with students challenges them to think critically, stimulates their imaginations, and encourages them to consider the nature of what it means to be human.

There is a wide range of subject matter, periods, styles, and structures in scripts teachers produce. Many are well-crafted examples of the artform, scripts that provide rich use of language, character, and structure. A number of scripts teacher-directors deem worthy for production because they provide opportunities for students in the company, and those in the audience, to grow emotionally, socially, and artistically. Plays with themes that are relevant to performers and audience members and with protagonists who live in the same world—or are challenged by the same concerns performers are facing—provide avenues for understanding self and others. Directors often note that production material related to students' lived experiences, whether classic or contemporary, while being relevant, shouldn't stoop to the derivative, sensational, contrived, or merely trendy. Instead, dramatic material that challenges the performer intellectually, emotionally, and artistically excites students to a greater understanding of the power of the theatrical form and the power of their voice within that form (Lazarus 1986).

Communities and schools have mostly unspoken standards of what is appropriate for students to perform and see. In addition to work that has artistic merit and student relevance, there are other criteria for choosing dramatic material. Depicting illegal and risky behaviors in the classroom or onstage without showing authentic consequences is neither honest nor socially responsible. With discussion and reflection, socially conscious theatre productions can reveal that drinking, drugging, being sexually active, and using weapons have consequences. If we produce plays or musicals in which fifteen-year-old girls play strippers or lovers to married men, or young boys play alcoholics or enact negative male stereotypes, are we not giving tacit approval to this behavior? Unless we show realistic consequences and discuss implications of negative behaviors, how will students understand the behaviors in a real-world context?

This is not to advocate for a season that has been purged of all controversial material. On the contrary, socially responsible programs actively tackle topics and productions that relate to the realities of students' lives, with teacher-artists handling controversial material in a responsible manner. (See Figure 3–4.)

Dramatic material that is age-appropriate may deal with difficult, controversial, or sensitive issues in a fashion that allows the audience members and performers to consider new perspectives and consequences for actions taken by the characters. Plays that raise questions or offer multiple perspectives on situations are intriguing to young people. Theatrical works need not resolve difficult issues or leave audiences with happy endings to be appropriate for study or performance.

Figure 3–4 *Working Responsibly with Controversial Material*

- Discuss assertions, assumptions, and stereotypes embedded in the text.

- Encourage students to think critically about the implications and consequences of characters' choices. Help students consider the characters' actions within the world of the play *and* within the real world.

- Look at the ideas the play presents from multiple perspectives and determine the production style and interpretation. Does it correlate with the story you and the students want to tell?

- Remember, you are neither a therapist nor a counselor. Include content specialists and trained social service, counseling, or mental health professionals as resources in your rehearsals and classes. Include professionals familiar with the issues presented in the play to help facilitate postperformance sessions.

- Make hotline information and resources readily available to company members if the topics being explored might affect students' mental, emotional, or physical health.

- Invite parents and administrators to open discussions about the play and your rationale for its selection.

- Alert parents and guardians to any incidents or discussions that concerned or upset students whether in the classroom or rehearsal. A letter, email, or call home allows everyone to be alert in caring for students' needs. Communicate with your principal about any such incidents and keep a record of that communication for yourself.

- Include dramaturgical information about the piece and the production in the program and/or in lobby displays.

- Schedule outreach sessions and prepare study materials about the play for classes in the school and for feeder schools who may be invited to see the play.

- Plan talkback sessions with the audience after each public performance. Prepare students to serve as dialogue facilitators.

Since socially responsible teacher-directors select scripts to produce for their own communities, there is not one set of rules that everyone follows. However, there are questions that may be helpful for teachers to consider when reviewing a script for production. (See Figure 3–5.)

Finding Time to Look for Material

Given the workload of most secondary school theatre teachers, finding age-appropriate dramatic material suitable for students can be a challenge; it takes time and it requires becoming familiar with a lot of scripts and talking to colleagues about their experiences with dramatic material. It can be tempting to produce only those scripts we have seen, directed before, or heard about from other teachers. To offset this temptation, teacher-directors I spoke with work with playwrights-in-residence, commission new works written specifically for their students, or take advantage of new play development projects through pro-

Figure 3–5 *Questions to Consider When Selecting a Script*

- Is there a relationship between the story being told in this script and my students, school, and community?

- What is the playwright's intent in terms of audience?

- Is the perspective presented that of a young person or an adult?

- Is the protagonist someone with whom young people can identify?

- Does the play respect the world of young people and respect the audience by presenting the material with artistry and depth?

- Will the imagination of young people in the audience be engaged? Will they engage intellectually and emotionally?

- Is the content such that the performers can understand it?

- Does the content relate to their life experiences in ways that they can recognize?

- Are there elements in the play that glamorize, trivialize, or promote risky, illegal, or morally questionable behavior without showing the consequences of such behaviors?

- Does the play respectfully address ideas relevant to diverse audiences and performers?

- Are the ideas in the play presented realistically, symbolically, metaphorically, or abstractly? Is this a style that can be accessible to young people? Can young people relate to the metaphors and symbols used?

- Are there aspects of the play that will need to be cut or edited to make it appropriate for the performers or audience? Can you get permission to make changes? What impact on the structure of the play will these changes make?

- Do I have concerns or doubts about the appropriateness of the material? (If so, have others read the play and pose your questions to them.)

fessional theatre education associations. Some involve students in play reading and/or play selection. Others have a regimen of reading a certain number of plays each month or over the summer. Some teacher-directors create a list of titles that they think would fit the students and the program in the coming year, and a student selection committee chooses from among these plays and determines the season. Other teachers, administrators, and parents are also sometimes involved.

This all takes time, but primarily it takes a willingness to do things differently. It means inviting students and teachers from throughout the school into dialogue. It may mean a teacher-artist acknowledging having limited knowledge of plays relevant to students whose ethnic, racial, and cultural backgrounds are different from his or her own, and then asking for help. It may mean wondering about students with disabilities, and then asking for their perspectives and ideas. It means, as Rebecca Jallings says,

> if there's something I don't understand about what . . . [students are] saying, what they're doing, I don't brush it off. I stop and say "Wait a minute, what does that mean? Explain that to me." Asking questions is an awful lot easier. (Jallings 2002)

Challenges to Socially Responsible Theatre Practice

> Don't let the hard boots of your idealism trample the tender shoots of your accomplishments.
> —GEORG LOCHER

Each community, school, and class, and each student within each class are constantly changing, and so must our responses to the issues and concerns we all face. Being socially engaged and responsive to the needs of students and the community can seem overwhelming in the face of the responsibilities of running a secondary school theatre program. I know at times I have lost my perspective and vision for a program or lost hope that the work was making any difference at all. Sometimes I have been challenged by others who have a different vision for my work. I am inspired by the attitudes that enable teacher-artists to continue in their journeys toward socially responsible theatre education. It helps me to remember that it is our own movement on the journey toward or away from best practice that should be considered. Figure 3–6 offers teacher-artist suggestions for facing these challenges.

Just as stars can guide sailors—though they are not trying to reach the stars—so our ideals can guide us even if they are unattainable.
—*David Darcy*, Teacher

Examples of Socially Responsible Practice

Conflict with Authority by Steve Bogart

Steve Bogart teaches near Boston, Massachusetts at Lexington High School. He is also a playwright and director. Socially responsible theatre education characterizes the program he and coteacher Sandy DiMartino have built at the school. In addition to their Drama of Social Issues class, they address social change and issues of interest to students in all of their courses. Conflict with Authority is a unit they use in their improvisation classes (Bogart 2003b).

Figure 3–6 *Embracing the Challenges of Socially Responsible Theatre Education*

- Be willing to begin and keep going. Do what you can.

- Remember that socially responsible work isn't just voicing or focusing on problems; it should raise questions and point to solutions and positive action.

- Don't be daunted by the skeptics, cynics, or naysayers.

- Don't be intimidated by the self-appointed champions for the rights of any group who criticize you in that "damned if you do and damned if you don't" way.

- Remember that education is messy.

- Don't be afraid of mistakes and missteps; they are inevitable.

- Have your own cause, talk about it, and be glad you don't have to make everyone else's cause your own.

- Be grateful that there are others willing to speak up about things they care about. Work with them to the extent you are headed in the same direction toward positive change.

- Remember everyone is on a different journey: find common ground; be inclusive and tolerant; work with people who think differently.

- Manage your time. Get out of the building and see daylight. Do something to care for *yourself* every day.

- Be patient on your journey and enjoy the view.

- Keep perspective. Not everything is an issue and not every issue can or needs to be addressed through theatre.

- Laugh. Find humor in your life and hope in your work.

JOURNAL ASSIGNMENT

A few days before the lesson, ask the students to:

Write about a conflict you have had with an authority figure.

Describe the situation, the setting, the background, and exactly what happened.

Write about something that you would be willing to share with the class.

THE LESSON

PARTNER UP AND SHARE YOUR STORIES. One student will be A and the other B. Pick one story to develop first. If it's A's story, B must play A. You must play the authority figure. You may not play yourself.

SHOW SCENES. Remember to look at what is behind the "villain's" attitude. What happened to make her or him feel this way? Change the scenes to [another] way they might have worked out, either fantastical or realistic. (**Note:** Consider doing three or four scenes before feedback.)

DISCUSS THE POSSIBLE MOTIVATION FOR THE AUTHORITY FIGURE AND CHILD TO RESPOND IN THE WAY THEY DID. Is the motivation based on something that happened in the past (internal) or is it an external motivation? External motivations come from without. A character's reaction to them is a choice under pressure. Internal motivations come from within and relates to a character's needs, desires, hopes, wishes, and dreams.

- List external motivations kids might have, for example: your parents have threatened to cut off your allowance if you don't have a B+ in English; the fire alarm goes off for a real fire; your friends pressure you not to hang out with the new kid.
- List possible external motivations adults might have: a really bad toothache; you lose your keys; your spouse leaves you and the kids; your child is lost.
- List internal motivations kids might have: you go to school even though you're sick because it's too hard to make up the work; you join a club to be closer to that cute guy or girl; you work for money to buy a car; you give up a friend because you are not having fun with her anymore.
- List internal motivations adults might have: you give up sleep to go to your daughter's game; you give up parts of your social life to advance your career; you begin an exercise program to get in shape.

SCENE: Create a scene in which we see an external motivation come into play for one or all of the characters. The choice they make in that moment will give us insight into the character.

PRESCENE: Choose one of the two authority figures (As and Bs) that you just worked with. Create a scene that shows what motivated your authority figure to behave the way that he did in the scene that we just saw. Create an external motivation for the character.

Consider the way people deal with external situations. Why do people make the choices that they make?

The Open Theatre by Jenny Lutringer

Jenny Lutringer teaches at Richland Hills High School near Fort Worth, Texas. Integrating study of avant-garde theatre with journal writing and discussions of current events and concerns in the students' lives, Jenny challenges students to use theatre as a catalyst for change and reflection. This unit is also learner-centered, as described in Chapter 2, and an example of Discipline Based Theatre Education as described in Chapter 4.

We ask them why people react so strongly to things, why someone might yell at a child or a young adult. . . . We have them do a scene showing what happened in the authority figure's life that [explains why] he or she might have reacted that strongly. . . . In a couple of different cases, kids have come to me and said "You know what, I never realized that when I came home drunk that night my mother was thinking about how she lost her best friend." . . . [A] student had a conflict with a guidance counselor, and the guidance counselor came to me and said "Are you doing that [conflict] lesson? Because the student actually came to me and apologized and said 'I know why I made you angry and I know why I did it now.'"

—Sandy DiMartino, Teacher

DAYS ONE, TWO, THREE: INTRODUCTION

Objectives

- Describe, analyze, interpret the work of The Open Theatre.
- See an example of the type of performance we will be developing.

THE IDEALS OF OPEN THEATRE   Explain that our next unit will be based on the work of the Open Theatre company.

We are going to create our own play like The Open Theatre created *The Serpent*. Over the next few days, keep your eyes open. Watch the news, read the newspaper, listen especially close in history class. We are going to take current events and respond to them through performance.

- Share several scenes from the videotape of *The Serpent* performed by The Open Theatre. After each scene stop and ask questions:

  What are the actors doing with their voices?

  How do the actors manipulate their bodies?

  What is this scene about?

  How does this scene relate to the previous scene(s)?

  What historical figures and events do you recognize?

  How do you think we view this differently today than the audience back then viewed it?

- Read excerpts from background materials packet about The Open Theatre.
- Discuss Joseph Chaikin and The Open Theatre process. Share language such as *representational* and *abstract* versus labels like *weird*.

Journal Questions

What do you want to tell an audience about the world you are living in today?

What current events have you found especially powerful lately? Why?

What commentary do you have on them?

ENSEMBLE EXERCISES.   Fine-tune skills students need to develop for this unit. After each exercise, tie it back to the ensemble nature of The Open Theatre. Following are a few sample games and exercises; the objective is to establish a basic vocabulary of *levels* and to show students the importance of level variation.

- Ask students to decide what levels correspond to what number. Level 1 is closest to the floor; 10 is highest from the floor.
- Play a game shouting out a number in which the students have to move instantly to that number, for example 1, 9, 2, 5. Challenge them on specifics: What is the difference between a 2 and a 3? a 9 and a 10?

- After this activity, we can easily evaluate a frozen statue and say if it needs a low or high number and why.

- Form group statues in response to words like *power, love, peace, despair.* This is done silently. Each group member must be at a different level and they are not allowed to discuss how to achieve this.

After playing these games and exercises, discuss:

Why do we need this knowledge of levels?

How is this way of creating frozen statues different than how we normally work?

How does the rule that everyone must be a different level aid this process? How does this relate to the process of The Open Theatre?

Variation: Do the same with movement and pace: 1 is slowest; 10 fastest. Repeat with volume: 1 is softest 10 is loudest.

[Jenny then has students do a series of give-and-take exercises with their bodies, voices, or visual art materials. She follows each movement, speaking, or drawing exercise with questions and ties their work back to that of The Open Theatre.]

DAYS THREE, FOUR, FIVE: INCORPORATING CURRENT EVENTS INTO ENSEMBLE WORK
Objectives

- Dissect newspaper articles and begin to realize the world around the articles.

- Represent the events and people in the article through frozen statues, gestures, and phrases.

- Decide what issues are to be incorporated into their scenes.

- Establish an approach to the scene work.

GROUP WORK   Students are divided into groups and given one article per class or per group to discuss. Articles are related to current events of interest in the lives of the students.

Discussion Questions

Who are the characters involved in this story?

Who is the victim? Perpetrator? Bystander?

Who are the characters involved that we might not see in the story?

What are the relationships among people?

What is the basic sequence of events?

BRINGING ARTICLES TO LIFE   Students remain in their groups and continue to work with the current article to create frozen statues.

Each person in the group assumes a different character from the situation suggested by the article. Different people (victim, perpetrator, bystander, etc.) should be represented. Ask students to stay with this character.

Ask students to chose or create one statement or phrase that is central to their character. The phrase can be from the article.

Ask students to create a gesture/movement to accompany the phrase. It might highlight the meaning or contrast ironically. (For example, a mother who lost her son might cry out 'My baby!" and either reach out for him or rock a child in her arms.)

Ask students to stand in a circle and share their phrases, going around the circle without stopping. Sidecoach students to use their entire bodies with their gestures and to use different levels. (*Variation*: Have everyone whisper their phrase, to build intensity.)

Ask students to break out of the circle and walk around the room freely. Say, "When I touch you on the shoulder, say your phrase and perform your gesture." Quicken the pace as it progresses, eventually allowing the students to say the phrases on their own. Sidecoach and work with students to get them to build to a climax of overlapping phrases and gestures until it explodes with a call to freeze in their original statues or to freeze one person at a time.

Ask students to create frozen statue(s) by showing one occurrence that might have led up to this event, and one occurrence that might happen years after this event, and one occurrence that happened at the climax of this event. Sidecoach students to use different levels to explore how they best can represent their characters physically and to show how the different characters relate to each other.

Ask students to share statues, one from each group. As you tap each character in the statue, the student should come alive, perform their gesture and line, and return to their frozen position. As the class describes, analyzes, and interprets the statues, have students identify who is playing what role. With the last group, perform a little experiment: assign an order to the students in the statue, have the students perform their gesture/phrase in order, and then ask the students to perform their gesture/phrase in that order four times in a row, building in volume and intensity from a whisper as they go.

Discussion Questions

Is this a performance?

How is this a performance?

How is this different from "traditional" scenework?

How does the lack of traditional dialogue affect the audience? How does the increase in volume affect the performance?

ESTABLISHING A CLASSROOM GOAL

[Jenny offers the following notes for establishing a classroom goal with students.]

- Take time to establish a goal with students and to select the issue or topic. This is crucial to the development of scenework and commitment to the project. Decide on the approach: Will each class produce one class performance? Will smaller groups within the class select their own topics and develop their own performances?

- Talk about being socially responsible. I share a quote from the film *Spider Man*, "With great power comes great responsibility." We talk about why we must be very careful when doing scenes based on real-life events, that not only should we be serious about our message, but we should respect the memory of any victims involved. I compare it to September 11th and how it would be to make a mockery of that event.

- Stress the ensemble nature of the performance. For example, we discuss that one person can play several parts because they are a neutral actor. This doesn't change the events or facts. It just is open-minded casting.

- Tie in a discussion of responsibility and integrity. The work of The Open Theatre was based on avant-garde performance that was more abstract and representational than realistic. Sometimes students get caught in wanting to show an actual event (shooting, killing, explosions) onstage. We also talk about how tragic events have been effectively staged over the centuries. I encourage them to consider adding meaning to the event representationally.

Discussion Questions

What do we want to say to the public?

What issue or theme do we want to develop our performance around?

Why is this article or issue important?

What kind of scenes do we want to develop over this issue?

How important is it to portray things accurately?

Can we change the events? the people involved?

Must a man play a man, or might a woman play the role?

How can we portray these events on stage? Must we do it realistically? Can we do it realistically?

Objectives

- Develop a series of scenes to be combined into a final performance.
- Incorporate performance techniques employed by The Open Theatre.
- Work with the group in an ensemble fashion.

Scenework as inquiry   Every day I pose a question to the class. The groups develop scenes to answer these questions. The same group(s) work with the same issue or event every day. I usually wait to create the next day's question until I see the students' work at the end of the day. The questions are my way of making sure they cover different perspectives that they might miss. I purposefully don't pose the questions in chronological order.

Discussion Questions

What is a solution to this problem?

What happened to cause this problem?

What commentary do you want to share?

What happened to the perpetrator to cause this event?

How did this event affect the victim's family?

How did the American public respond to this event?

Create a scene to address the question. Within each scene, incorporate the following:

- nontraditional movement (slow motion; breaking movement into steps; frozen statues; repetition; being a machine or animal)
- nontraditional dialogue (songs, humming, making a noise, repetition, monotone, narration of a scene as it happens, speeches, headlines/quotes, numbering)
- historical facts, figures, events about real events and people
- repetition of a theme or imagery to connect scenes (what it means to be proven guilty, patriotic songs underscoring different events). One group connected the Buddhists who set themselves on fire because of religious persecution to the Jews whose dead bodies were burned during the Holocaust. They then interjected Joan of Arc being burned at the stake. Underneath it all, connecting the different historical figures, was a girl reciting a poem about the fiery flames of injustice that attack those who are different.
- breaking of the fourth wall/integration of the audience (dumping a barrel of apples into the audience and inviting them to eat, choosing audience

members to serve as jury members in a scene, kicking someone out of their seat, pointing at the audience and pronouncing them guilty, demanding the audience stand and recite the Pledge of Allegiance)

- chorus section (Create a scene that comments on this situation from outside)

Jenny offers an example of how the Scenework as Inquiring phase of her unit was developed by students.

> This year at Richland [High School], the class decided to choose one theme/idea [injustice] and have all groups combine into one large class performance. . . . Every day we would choose a new event. Each group would choose a different aspect of the event to portray, a different question to respond to over the same issue. One group was assigned to the chorus section . . . [which] is meant as a commentary versus a "scene." . . . The chorus [section is] performed several times, and changed only slightly. This allowed the audience to really absorb their message. (2002a)

At the end of each day, we share, critique, and rework our scenes.

Discussion Questions

How do these scenes connect together?

What things might we incorporate to strengthen this connection? (This is a good time to work with any students who are hesitant to embrace the abstract nature of the work.)

How might you rework your scene to make it less realistic?

What will this add to the meaning?

What are the benefits of a nontraditional performance like this?

FINAL PERFORMANCE PREPARATIONS

Objective

- Combine previous scenes through transitions.
- Prepare for a final presentation/performance.
- Effectively use transitions to maintain the flow and intensity of the piece.

PUTTING THE SCENES TOGETHER Share two scenes that will be performed back to back.

Discussion Questions

What happened at the end of the scene?

What happened to the audience at this point?

How can we keep both the actors engaged and the audience still interested? (We discuss the fact that once the performance starts, the student is performing the entire time. There shouldn't be a break in character.)

How can performing transitions highlight your message? (Students offer examples.) All scenes should be linked in this way. Give students a day or two to work on transitions.

As a class, we then establish an order of scenes, we write it on the board, and revise it as necessary.

Objectives

Perform final piece.
Perform all scenes without breaking the performance.
Connect own work with the work of their peers.
Describe, analyze, and interpret own work and the work of their peers.

On the day of the performance, remind students of the scene order established the day before. Allow a three-to-five minute brushup rehearsal; set area for performance; perform. (Note: For the first full performance, I do not invite an audience. Many times the students are shocked at the impact of their work and they need to debrief alone, as a class.)

Pre- and Postperformance Questions

How might this performance impact an audience differently than a traditional performance? than a documentary?

How are you, the actor, impacted differently than from other types of work?

What is the impact of combining this wide assortment of events from our past into one performance?

What connects these events?

What separates them?

How does this type of work compare and contrast to a poem? a piece of literature? a history book? a movie? a song?

Throughout the process students are encouraged to share their personal responses in their discussions, journals, and in conversations with each other and Jenny.

Ideas for Further Reflection

What Is, What Could Be, and What Ought to Be My Socially Responsible Practice?

LOOK AT WHAT IS

What is the current relationship of your theatre program to the people and activities in the rest of your school and community? Invite colleagues, parents, students, business leaders, or others into your conversations as appropriate.

- In what ways is my program representative of the students in my school? In what ways is it not?

- In what ways is my classroom and my program inviting and accessible to all of the students in the school?

- Is the material I teach and produce age-appropriate? In what ways isn't it? How does the material I teach and produce relate to the lives of my students? In what ways do I make that connection consciously? How am I "teaching to transfer?"

- What are the obstacles I face in finding appropriate material? How can I overcome these obstacles?

- How do I characterize my interactions and communications with students? With coteachers? With parents and administrators? With others involved with my program? With those in the communities served by the school? Who might be a partner with me?

- How often do I interact with people who are not in my program?

- If I could make one positive change in my professional relationships, what would I do?

- What links are there between what I do in my program and the rest of the school, the community, and the world? What links would I like to have?

- How does my teaching philosophy reflect my views of socially responsible practice?

- What would a handbook for my program contain? Would new students reading it feel included and clear about how to be involved? How would they find out what the acceptable behaviors with peers and adults are?

- What is my district's censorship policy? Does it address issues that might arise in my program? Who might help me draft a policy regarding censorship?

Look at *What Should Be*

Consider the kind of community you want to have in your theatre program. Look back at the lists you made at the end of Chapter 1 and revisit your vision of the theatre education community in which you most want to work.

- In what ways can we create a safe place to take risks and experiment in this program?

- How can people from different cultural backgrounds, races, genders, religions, sexual orientations, languages, and abilities interact with each other?

- How can people express their individuality?

- How can we deal with "problem" individuals? (What *is* a problem individual?)

- How do we care for each other?
- How do we give each other feedback?
- How do we respond when we become aware of differences?

LOOK AT *WHAT WILL BE*

Take your vision of a socially responsible theatre program and think about examples from this chapter and from other teachers and artists you have seen or read about. Begin a plan of action to effect positive change in your program and school.

How Did I Come To Think This Way?

Jot down your response to the following questions. Think about how these experiences might shape your thinking and perspectives of yourself, colleagues, parents, and students. How do you see your thinking affecting your practice?

- What did your parents teach you about your race, religion, gender, sexual orientation, culture, heritage, language, abilities, socioeconomic status? What did they teach you about people who were different from you?
- Are you proud to be your race, gender, socioeconomic status? Do you still practice customs and cultural events that are connected to your identity?
- Has there ever been an incident in your family or a conflict because of one of these areas of difference?
- How many people who are different from you in terms of socioeconomic status, race, language, religion, culture, gender, sexual orientation, or abilities/disabilities do you interact with regularly?
- What is the most difficult area of difference you face? What areas of difference do you find difficult when interacting with students or other adults? How might this affect your practice? What action might you take to address this difficulty?
- Who can you go to with questions?

Make a plan to address your questions and to learn more about difference. Make a plan for your classes and productions and other aspects of your program. Be willing to be "on the ice" (Schroeder-Arce 2002a).

Selected Resources

There are many excellent resources on topics addressed in this chapter. In addition to the works cited in the chapter, the following offer ideas for further reflection.

Delpit, Lisa. 1995. *Other People's Children: Cultural Conflict in the Classroom*. New York: The New Press.

Donkin, Ellen, and Susan Clement, eds. 1993. *Upstaging Big Daddy: Directing Theater as if Gender and Race Matter.* Ann Arbor: The University of Michigan Press.

Lanoux, Carol, and Elizabeth O'Hara. 1999. "Deconstructing Barbie: Using Creative Drama as a Tool for Image Making in Pre-Adolescent Girls." *Stage of the Art* 10 (3).

Noddings, Nell. 1984. *Caring: A Feminine Approach to Ethics and Moral Education.* Berkley: University of California Press.

Payne, Ruby 1995. *Poverty: A Framework for Understanding and Working with Students and Adults from Poverty.* Baytown, TX: RFT Publishers.

Ressler, Paula. 2002. *Dramatic Changes: Talking About Sexual Orientation and Gender Identity with High School Students Through Drama.* Portsmouth, NH: Heinemann.

Romo, Harriett, D., and Toni Falbo. 1996. *Latino High School Graduation: Defying the Odds.* Austin: University of Texas Press.

Saldaña, Johnny. 1995. *Drama of Color: Improvisation with Multiethnic Folklore.* Portsmouth, NH: Heinemann.

Tatum, Beverly Daniel. 1999. *"Why Are All the Black Kids Sitting Together in the Cafeteria?" And Other Conversations About Race.* New York: Basic Books.

Note

1. Jacquelyn Woodson's *From the Notebooks of Melanin Sun,* won the Coretta Scott King Award when it was published in 1996.

4 *Comprehensive Theatre Education*

Theatre is everywhere in our society . . . except in the typical preK–12 curriculum. Relatively few comprehensive sequential theatre education programs exist in the United States. . . . If substantial programs are ever to exist, theatre must be perceived as an academic discipline relevant to all students rather than an extracurricular activity for a selected few. The teaching of theatrical knowledge and skills through the inherent processes of theatre can result in an appreciation of the complexity of the art form, recognition of its existence in all cultures throughout history, and understanding of its power and relevance in today's global society.

—Kim Wheetley, Southeast Center for Education in the Arts

When my son was little, he regularly engaged in pretend play. He moved easily in and out of the roles of director, performer, designer, playwright, critic, and audience. "OK, mom, wear this hat and stand like this—over there by the fort [the sofa]—and when I take out my sword you flip on the light and say 'Who goes there?'" He would then critique my character interpretation and help me understand my motivation, all the while revising my lines. Admittedly, his preschool approach to theatre was more egocentric and dogmatic than learner-centered, but even now that he is older, he and his friends still think of theatre, and life for that matter, holistically. They do not see the world in which they live as fragmented into subjects and disciplines.

This chapter explores models of theatre education that allow children to see and experience their world holistically, and foster in them a desire to inquire, experience, define, and reflect on the world fully and from multiple perspectives. Neil Postman describes it:

> What children need is a curriculum that would have at its core the drama of knowledge; a curriculum that would allow children to create meaning from disparate and disconnected facts that fill the world . . . a curriculum that would convey the idea that all life is a drama—an improvisation, if you will—in which the point is not to make things happen but to make meaningful things happen. (Postman 1990, 6)

The importance of a comprehensive approach to theatre education is clear to me as I observe preservice teachers in schools. A couple of years ago I observed a student teaching a vocal unit to a high school theatre class; she was having students echo her as she recited the lyrics from a Gilbert and Sullivan patter song. Some of the students were obediently parroting her, though many were distracted, distracting others, doing the exercise in a detached manner, or doing it without proper breath support or articulation. This appeard to be a classroom management problem. As I continued to watch, however, I found myself thinking that I, too, would be uninterested in this activity. Why were the students being asked to do it? They weren't studying Gilbert and Sullivan, and there were no curricular or cultural links to the text. They weren't being asked to think about or interact with the material or each other, and they were not enjoying it. These vocal activities were not even warming anyone up to participate.

Both the student teacher and I learned something about best practice that day. I was reminded that at one time I led warm-ups and taught vocal and movement exercises that were not linked to what was being studied or rehearsed. There was little connection among activities within a lesson or across curricular units. I was teaching theatre in the same disconnected way I had been taught, which was the same way my teachers and their teachers had been taught. Not surprisingly, students weren't transferring the knowledge and skills being taught to their other work in class or onstage. I critically examined some of my teaching methods and discovered that disjointed, compartmentalized study of theatre actually thwarts many students in their growth as artists, thinkers, scholars, or citizens. Development, application, and transfer of knowledge need to be linked together and embedded in a comprehensive study of theatre. This approach engages students in learning and results in not mere acquisition of information but *understanding* and the ability to *apply* that understanding in class and onstage.

Rather than separate instructional units about acting, play analysis, or lighting, what might a larger study of theatre look like? The teachers I spoke with engage students in learning theatre history, production, and criticism. Their students create original work and talk easily about the style, its historical roots, its meaning, and the art and craft necessary for its creation. In many schools, the arts teachers talk and work together, developing curricula and pursuing joint projects. Some theatre teachers integrate their curricula with teachers from other academic departments. All totaled, this is *comprehensive theatre education*. It is an interwoven study and exploration of all aspects of theatre. It encompasses a core of holistic study of the theatre disciplines and then expands and intersects with work across other arts disciplines and academic areas (see Figure 4–1).

> In my definition, comprehensive means all-inclusive. It also implies balance—of kinds of activities, experiential approaches, instructional methods, ranges of art forms, types of instructors, ethnicity, cultural values and the like.
>
> —Jane Remer

Discipline-Based Theatre Education: A Framework for Learning

Knowing that comprehensive theatre education is "an interwoven study and exploration of all aspects of theatre" is fine—but how is interwoven study created? What does it look like?

There are any number of ways to conceptualize comprehensive education in theatre. Discipline-Based Theatre Education[1] (DBTE) is one example of a

Figure 4–1 *Comprehensive Theatre Education*

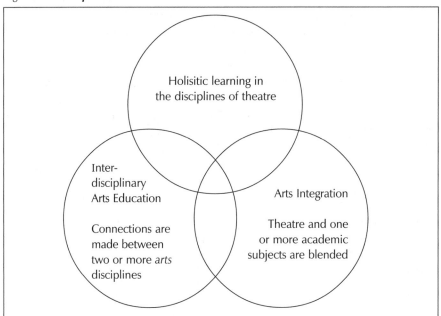

Holisitic learning in the disciplines of theatre

Inter-disciplinary Arts Education

Connections are made between two or more *arts* disciplines

Arts Integration

Theatre and one or more academic subjects are blended

> If the theatre walls could be glass instead of concrete then people could see in and hear. And conversely the people inside could look out [so they are not] isolated and not just in their own black box, in their own created world and not anyone's reality.
>
> —*Kim Wheetley*

conceptual framework teachers use when developing curriculum and designing lessons. DBTE is a clear articulation of holistic education in theatre; it integrates many instructional approaches, providing "a variety of strategies for experiencing, understanding, reflecting upon, and valuing works of theatre and the theatre process" (Wheetley and SCEA 1996).

The Discipline-Based Theatre Education framework is structured for students' active exploration of theatre through eight theatrical roles (see Figure 4–2), and four methods of inquiry, through which students investigate these theatrical roles (see Figure 4–3). This results in an interwoven and comprehensive theatre education (see Figure 4–4) allowing students to learn about theatre from multiple perspectives.

STUDENTS IN DBTE PROGRAMS

Comprehensive theatre education is inherently socially responsible and learner-centered. Instructional experiences are also *authentic*, meaning students gain the kinds of skills and knowledge needed to participate in various theatre professions. Students read, create, perform, and attend works of theatre. They interpret and derive meaning about their lives and the lives of people from worldwide cultures, past and present. Additionally, students work across other disciplines and interact with professional artists at school and in the community. Student assessment and evaluation reflect the comprehensive and varied nature of their study.

Autumn Samsula Casey uses the DBTE framework for a unit in her advanced theatre class. Her high-school students have an integrated experience in theatre

Figure 4–2 *Disipline-Based Theatre Education Conceptual Framework*

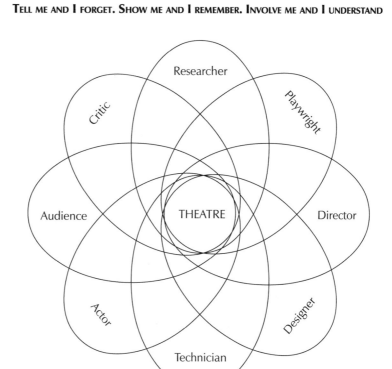

TELL ME AND I FORGET. SHOW ME AND I REMEMBER. INVOLVE ME AND I UNDERSTAND

Researcher

Playwright

Critic

THEATRE

Audience

Director

Actor

Designer

Technician

Students understand theatre holistically by connecting and blending their experiences in the eight theatrical roles.

© Southeast Center for Education in the Arts, 1996

history, research, text analysis, dance, acting, criticism, and costume design and construction. They learn about Elizabethan history while exploring themes from one of Shakespeare's plays, which Autumn correlates with events in their lives. In later lessons, students learn about Elizabethan culture, see how clothing of the period was made, and experience how the clothes enhance or constrict movement while learning the Allemande. They conduct research, do text work, and use costumes to rehearse and perform scenes from the play. Criticism and aesthetics are integrated throughout (Casey 2003).

Two of my former students chose a comprehensive approach when they taught costume design and technology as part of their preservice education. Using a process drama structure, the student teachers introduced a crime for which the only clues were articles of clothing. Acting as detectives, students looked at each article of clothing for clues about suspects. They researched period costumes, drew sketches, wore the clothing, and took on the roles of characters suggested through their

Figure 4–3 *Learning Theatre Through Methods of Inquiry*

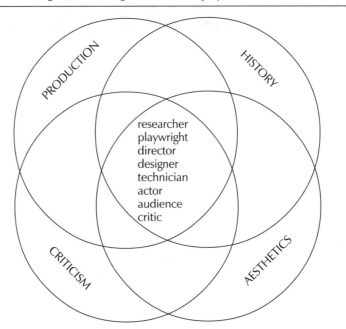

PRODUCTION   HISTORY   CRITICISM   AESTHETICS

researcher
playwright
director
designer
technician
actor
audience
critic

Work in production, history, criticism, and aesthetics unifies theatre study and challenges students to make meaningful connections between the eight theatrical roles.

Students

- create informal and formal theatre by researching, improvising, writing, designing, constructing, rehearsing, and performing (production)

- consider theatre in social, cultural, and historical contexts (history)

- reflect on the aesthetic qualities and characteristics of theatre (aesthetics)

- make informed judgments about the theatre they create and experience (criticism) (Wheetley and SCEA 1996)

research. The unit included opportunities for students to enact the events leading up to the crime and the arrests.

When Deb Alexander (1999) learned of the DBTE framework she became intrigued by the thought of using it as a springboard for a middle school theatre curriculum. As discussed in Chapter 1, Deb adapted the framework by using *The Diary of Anne Frank* as the core through which the four methods of inquiry and eight theatrical roles would all intersect. Students explored the themes, events, and ideas of the play in a sequenced, interactive, and holistic semester-long class. Excerpts from Deb's curriculum are included at the end of this chapter on pages 114–133.

Figure 4–4 *The Theatrical Weaving*

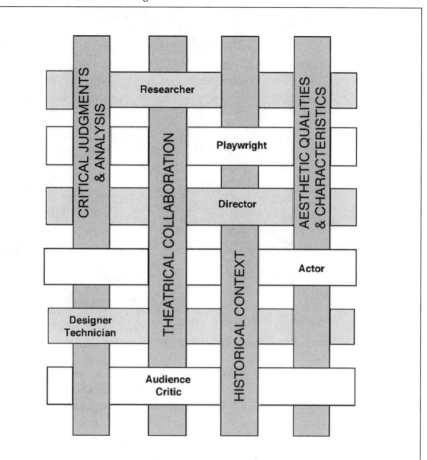

Given a program that incorporates a strong foundation of theatrical components, a balance of learning opportunities, and dynamic instruction, teachers and students can weave an exquisite and enduring discipline-based theatrical tapestry.

© Southeastern Center for Education in the Arts, 1996

Jenny Lutringer's (2002a, 2003a) unit in Chapter 3 on The Open Theatre is an example of effective comprehensive theatre education—a comprehensive, learner-centered, and socially engaged unit (see pages 93–100).

Coteaching in Comprehensive Theatre Education

Although many teachers are the only theatre professional in their school offering comprehensive theatre education for students, when there are two or more theatre teachers in a school there is the opportunity to blend classes, team teach, or

Figure 4–5 *Student dramaturgs work on an upcoming production.*

© Southeastern Center for Education in the Arts, 1996

coteach. Diane Stewart (2002) and another theatre teacher in her school joined their two ninth-grade theatre classes to address Shakespeare, Elizabethan history, culture, and voice. Other teachers regularly integrate curricula, exchange classes, coteach, or codirect. Modeling the collaborative nature of theatre, they share their individual and collective knowledge with all of the students.

Interdisciplinary Arts Education

> Disciplinary integration in art is educationally desirable not only because it represents the actual ways in which artists and arts-related professionals experience art, but because it is an effective way to underscore and reinforce what is important.
>
> —STEPHEN MARK DOBBS

> Interdisciplinary curriculum should be an expansion of, not a substitute for, a sequential comprehensive curriculum in each subject discipline.
>
> —CONNECTICUT GUIDE TO INTERDISCIPLINARY CURRICULUM DEVELOPMENT

Professional artists have long challenged boundaries among arts disciplines. It is important to students' comprehensive study of theatre that they too have opportunities to challenge and experience the similarities, differences, and authentic intersections between art forms. Comprehensive theatre education includes meaningful curricular and cocurricular experiences in which theatre is integrated with one or more of the other arts disciplines. Teachers incorporate work from different art forms in specific units of study in their classrooms, work in a cross-disciplinary fashion in productions, or develop special interdisciplinary projects in the school or community.

Some theatre teachers also teach English classes, and regularly integrate the disciplines of literature and theatre. JoBeth Gonzalez (2002b), for instance, teaches *Julius Caesar* in her sophomore English classes. In a single lesson she draws correlations among the play, Greek history, current events, and students' lives. She then integrates exploration of the text with exploration of acting style, enactment of scenes, and a discussion of the work from critical and feminist perspectives. Misty Valenta (2002) created a drama lesson in which she drew on music, movement, and drama to engage students in exploration of events and themes from the novel *Watership Down*.

Carol Cain teaches at West Side School, a grades 3–8 arts magnet program in LaGrange, Georgia. The school uses a Discipline-Based Interdisciplinary Arts Education approach. Carol feels there are enormous benefits that come from working with other arts educators who teach through and across the arts.

> The beauty of where I work is that I gain total inspiration from the visual art and the music teacher that I work with. And that . . . is a strong part of what I feel is . . . our success. That's been probably the best part of this job for me . . . , working with [my arts colleagues]. And many of the plans that we've developed we did together. (Cain 2003)

She describes how integrating theatre into her middle school English classes has benefited her students.

> We were going over . . . two hundred vocabulary words we'd learned during the semester . . . . When I'd call out a word . . . they'd kind of stumble around until somebody said "Oh yeah, it means blah blah blah." . . . I got to this one set of words, and I called them and they knew every single one of them. "How do you all know those words so well?" "Oh, Miss Cain, don't you remember? Those are the ones we did the drama scenes with." I went "Oh, yeah." . . . They had written, and of course, performed their own scenes using the vocabulary words, and obviously they remembered them. (2003)

Teachers also collaborate on productions with colleagues in art, music, and dance. Bradford High School in Kenosha, Wisconsin, is an example of a school in which the arts faculty jointly develop interdisciplinary curriculum and performances. In addition to regular classes offered in each arts discipline, the productions are mounted through classes for which students register and receive credit. These theatre practicum classes are held after school or in the evening to allow as many students as possible to participate. Holly Stanfield (2002) heads the performing arts program in the school. When the program started, Holly was employed two-thirds time teaching one theatre class and one television class. The curriculum and the program grew with student interest and support from the principal and school board. She now collaborates with six other colleagues in music, theatre, English, and television. All of them teach classes and direct; together they teach theatre practicum, encouraging students to explore connections across the arts.

Most teachers who integrate the arts do so alone, within their own classrooms or productions. However, there are now national initiatives urging arts integration and collaboration among teacher–artists from different disciplines.[2] Teachers doing interdisciplinary arts codesign curriculum, coplan lessons, or team teach with other arts colleagues. In some programs, theatre teachers also serve as guests and specialists for classes of other disciplines or as a resource to colleagues in other fields. A number of teachers I spoke with who have not yet moved in these directions expressed a desire to do so.

Arts Integration

> We may learn much about human behavior through social studies, literature, and science, but drama requires that we *feel* our way *into* the situations of others. . . . Many educators do not seem to understand that drama is a way of knowing—and often a more stimulating way than that offered through the distanced learning provided in a purely intellectual approach.
>
> —Oscar G. Brockett

A number of theatre teachers find that integrating their curriculum with other school subjects makes learning more engaging for those already attracted to theatre. It also makes theatre more accessible to a wider range of students. Integrating the arts across the curriculum can also positively impact an entire school.

> When New York's Educational Priorities Panel (Connell 1996) studied a group of struggling inner-city elementary schools that raised their standardized test scores dramatically and got off the city's academic "probation" list, panel researchers made a surprising discovery. Even though probation status focused urgent attention on the "basic" reading and math content appearing on achievement tests, many of the schools that got off the list had actually *increased* their arts programming. "These successful schools," the report said, "were distinguished by a strong arts program that was infused through the instructional program and that included most of the students in the school." (Zemelman, Daniels, and Hyde 1998, 161–62)

Infusion is but one approach to integrating the arts with nonarts disciplines. There may be as many variations on arts integration as there are teachers engaged in its practice. The following examples show teacher-artists integrating theatre with the broader school curriculum to effectively reach and teach students across the school population.

In their book *Dramatic Literacy*, J. Lea Smith and J. Daniel Herring (2001) describe potential intersections in the middle school curriculum among theatre and literature, science, mathematics, and second language learning, and illustrate the benefits of integrated learning across the curriculum for middle-school students.

> Drama creates a setting where a person is able to explore and experiment with content through self-perception, social interaction, movement, and language—reading, writing, speaking, and listening. Integrating drama into content studies provides the middle-level learner with a learning environment which supports their developmental needs for voice and ownership in the learning process. (xi–xii)

Other teachers collaborate with colleagues and develop units of study that they coteach in some fashion. As part of her MFA thesis project, Rebecca Schlomann (2004) designed a pilot unit that integrates theatre with the mentorship program Peer Assistance and Leadership (PALs).[3] The centerpiece of the unit is development of a theatre-in-education (TIE) piece through which students achieve the objectives of both the theatre and PALs curricula. Rebecca first looked at the curriculum for each subject for correlations of goals and objectives. She then looked at her teaching style and methodologies and those of the PALs teacher. She found ways in which their styles complimented and overlapped each other and built lesson plans and evaluation strategies from this information.

Successfully Collaborating with Colleagues

Working with other teachers and artists means negotiating territory, resources, boundaries, work styles, and work ethics. My most rewarding and my most troublesome teaching and artmaking experiences can be linked directly to the unique demands of collaboration. Whether in joyful or agonizingly difficult projects, the joy or trouble almost always stemmed from what happened, or didn't happen, *before* the project began. How much preparation, communication, negotiation, shared understanding, and investment were in place before we started had a direct impact on how well the project went. The outcomes can also be linked to how willing everyone was to relinquish some control and to let others share leadership. With each new endeavor, I learn more about dealing with change graciously. I am learning that different is not always bad and that new can be exciting. I am also learning that harboring unspoken expectations is a luxury I cannot afford when young people are involved. I have to communicate with colleagues clearly, early, and often. I need to explain what my students need, what our boundaries are, what I can give to the project, and what I can't. I must be willing also to listen to what my colleagues are saying. We will then best serve all of our students.

Tips for designing successful collaborative projects were gleaned from my conversations with teachers and artists (see Figure 4–6). While by no means a complete list, these suggestions are a resource for your journey toward best practice.

Figure 4–6 *Tips for Successful Collaborations*

- Initiate conversations with colleagues in theatre, music, art, dance, and other disciplines. Get to know them and their interests.

- Find common ground. Look for ways in which you and your colleagues might share:
  - an interest in collaborating;
  - a vision for the school;
  - respect for and commitment to students; and
  - common curricular objectives or methodologies.

- Seek out and work with people who are open to problem solving and who tolerate divergent thinking.

- Develop a willingness to change how things have been done in the past, how schedules are arranged, how units are taught and by whom.

- Devote time for collaborative planning. Remember to plan assessments and evaluations that reflect work in each discipline as well as integrated knowledge and skills.

- Be honest about how much time you can invest.

- If possible, start small. Do pilot or short-term projects with clear beginnings and endings.

- Don't expect to have all of the answers or the best answers all of the time.

- Expect to make mistakes. Learn from everyone's mistakes.

- Prepare students. Tell them what you anticipate will happen in collaborations with other teachers or guest artists. Assure them that some things will change, that there will be surprises, and that you are looking out for their best interest. (Be sure that you are.) Let students know that they can come to you with questions, concerns, and discoveries.

- Hindsight is 20/20. Take what you learn in each project, especially what worked well, and let that propel you into the next project. Focusing only on what didn't work doesn't foster progress.

- Be patient. Find and cherish the small successes and build on them.

An Example of Comprehensive Theatre Education

A Drama-Based Interdisciplinary Model by Deb Alexander

As discussed on page 108 and in Chapter 2, Deb Alexander's curriculum model engages students in learner-centered and holistic theatre education. While developed for middle school students, the lessons and structure easily lend themselves to work with high schoolers. Deb explains how her design process gives context to her adaptation of the DBTE model: "Model A is based on the . . . [SCEA] model. At the center . . . however is a play from which the different theatrical roles stem and interconnect" (1999, 7). (See Figure 4–7.)

Figure 4–7   *Model A: Drama-Based Interdisciplinary Model*

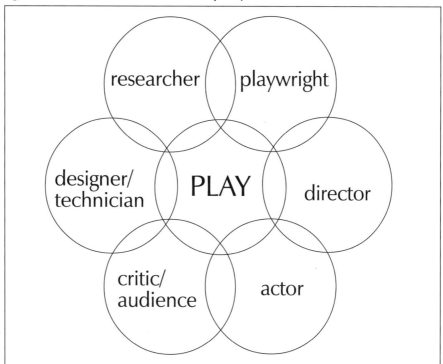

In this design, the teacher has placed a play at the core of the curriculum. The play serves as a link between the methods of inquiry and the perspectives.

© Alexander 1999

Deb explains, "Model B . . . shows how the six roles from Model A can be applied to exploration of the text. "The first four steps are a process through which students learn tools and build the foundation necessary to create a final product in Step Five" (see Figure 4–8). To illustrate her model, Deb used *The Diary of Anne Frank*, originally adapted by Frances Goodrich and Albert Hackett (1958) (1999, 8). Deb goes on to explain how Models A and B work in practice:

> For the first six weeks, students are introduced to the core material by exploring key issues in the play and reading and analyzing the script using various drama techniques. The next two weeks are designed to help students ask questions and to learn alternative means of research through the exploration of oral histories, Internet sites, visual art works, and other library resources. The next four weeks are dedicated to the design process as students transform the classroom into a workshop to explore scenic, costume, lighting, and sound design. The final six weeks are reserved for students to produce specific scenes from the script. They . . . create a theatre company and share their work with an invited audience at the end of the term. . . . The primary focus is on student development and learning leading to a production of selected scenes versus a production of a play as the primary objective. (1999, 9–10)

Figure 4–8 *Model B: Curriculum Sequence*

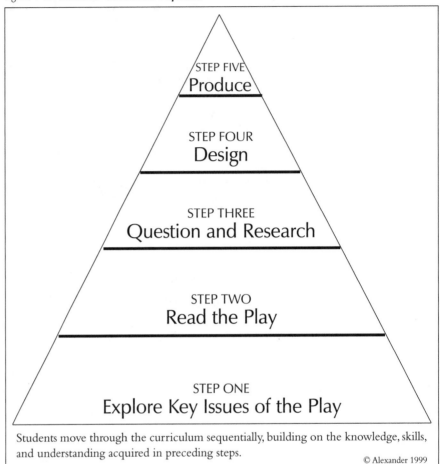

STEP FIVE
Produce

STEP FOUR
Design

STEP THREE
Question and Research

STEP TWO
Read the Play

STEP ONE
Explore Key Issues of the Play

Students move through the curriculum sequentially, building on the knowledge, skills, and understanding acquired in preceding steps.

© Alexander 1999

[Not wanting to dilute the history presented in *The Diary of Anne Frank* by covering too much material, Deb selected three themes or issues to explore: oppression, survival, and hope. The following selected lessons combine the steps in Model B with those themes for the semester-long class.]

Step One: Exploring the Issues

OPPRESSION

Methodology

- group discussion
- theatre games
- role drama
- debate

Focus

What is stereotyping and how does it affect our everyday lives?

Materials

- soup can without a label
- National Geographic on Assignment: USA
- Star of David
- Holocaust Photo
- butcher paper
- tape
- markers

Student Objectives

- Identify and define what a stereotype is.
- Explore the consequences of stereotyping by playing the roles of the victim, perpetrator, and bystander.
- Debate in two groups the fate of one victim by examining the pros and cons of their personal choice.

Lesson and Content Structure

- Show students the can without the label.

    What could be in this can?

    How are we able to identify its contents?

    What other kinds of labels exist? (example: clothing)

    What do labels say about a person?

    How do we label people in our lives?

    How do we label ourselves?

- Share photos of everyday people.

    Describe this person in one word.

    How can one word describe someone?

- Write the word *stereotype* on the board.

    How do we stereotype in our everyday lives, and why?

    What are the consequences?

    How are teenagers stereotyped by adults?

    Why are they stereotyped?

    What is the result?

ACTIVITY: CREATE A COMMUNITY   Everyone walk around the room in your own space as yourself. Change directions. Head for open space. Create a community of people who are like you according to the specific instructions that the leader calls out. (For example, "Create a community of people who are like you from the waist down." All students who are wearing jeans might create a group while those who are wearing skirts might create another group.)

Create a community of people who are like you:
> neck up
>
> ankles down
>
> neck down waist up

What is the name of your community? Break up and walk around. Create a community of people who are like you. (Continue at least three times.)

Variation

> Find people who are the same (offer internal vs. physical characteristics) (examples: favorite movie, brothers/sisters, music).

Discussion

> What is a community?
>
> How do you choose who is in your community and who is not?
>
> In this exercise, when did things get difficult in figuring out who was in your community and who was not?
>
> In your school or neighborhood, who is in your community?
>
> What happens when someone doesn't belong to a community?

Other Questions

> How does stereotyping play into creating a community?
>
> What are the dangers of stereotyping?

ACTIVITY: RUMOR MILL   There is a new kid at school who is not like you. In pairs, talk about this new student. They are not like you. How are they different? Move into groups of four and share the information that you have heard so far about the new student.

Discussion

> How does stereotyping play into spreading rumors?
>
> What are the dangers of spreading rumors?

ACTIVITY: CHILD/PARENT ROLE PLAY   Divide the class into pairs. Each pair will improvise a situation that the new student might experience. Share selected short scenes with the class and discuss.

Situation One

Child: You want to go outside and play in your new neighborhood.

Parent: You don't want your child to go out—try to keep them safe.

Situation Two

Child: You don't want to go to school, especially after the events that occurred due to the rumor mill.

Parent: Try to convince your child why it's so important that they go to school.

ACTIVITY: STUDENT'S FATE   Show the picture of Star of David and other "labels" that the Nazis used to define their prisoners. Say, "For the next several weeks, we will be exploring a period of history called the Holocaust, where stereotyping played a major role in the death and destruction of several races of people due to the discrimination of a select few who thought themselves superior to everyone else."

Discussion

Should the student continue going to this school or transfer?
  List Pros and Cons.

How do you define stereotyping?

How does stereotyping lead to discrimination?

How can we fight discrimination?

SURVIVAL

Methodology

- image theatre
- group discussion

Focus

What do humans need to exist happily?

Materials

- handout
- chalkboard and chalk
- chronology worksheet

Figure 4–9 *Rights and Freedoms Worksheet*

Think of the freedom that the following rights afford you and your family. Think of the ways you and your family would be affected if these rights were revoked. Remember, if these rights were revoked, this would mean giving up things you already have.

Rank these rights from 1 to 6—1 being **MOST** important to you.

The Right to:

___ own or use a public telephone

___ date/marry whomever you choose

___ own a radio, CD player, TV

___ own a pet

___ go to a movie or rock concert

___ leave your house whenever you choose (You would still be able to leave the house, but there would be strict limitations on when you could go out.)

Student Objectives

- Create a Hierarchy of Needs similar to Maslow's Hierarchy of Needs.
- Examine the chronology of decrees that revoked the rights of the Jewish population.
- Discuss the impact of these laws on the individual based on their needs (social, emotional, physical).
- Create individual and group frozen images describing what makes them happy and the consequences of that happiness taken away.

Lesson and Content Structure

- Distribute Rights and Freedoms worksheet for students to complete independently (see Figure 4–9). Have students work in small groups to discuss their decisions. Each group works to come to a consensus and ranks the rights as a group. Small-group responses and rationales are shared and discussed.
- Discuss the laws that revoked the rights of individuals during the time peroid of the play. For an excellent reference with a complete chronology of the period, see the novel *Frederich* by Hans Peter Richter (Richter 1987).

ACTIVITY: CREATE FROZEN STATUES Discuss the ways an individual would be affected through the revoking of rights and freedoms. Students work in pairs, using their bodies to describe their thoughts and feelings.

1. One student is the sculptor and the other is the clay. The sculptor molds the clay into a frozen statue of an activity that makes them happy. (examples: playing baseball, talking on the phone)

2. Next, the sculptor molds the clay into a frozen statue of how they feel when the activity they enjoy is taken away. (examples: frustration, anger)

3. Have the statues start out in the first image and slowly transform to the second image with an eight count.

4. Have the sculptors sit down in the audience and observe the two statues in transformation. Choose specific statues that stand out for the students to discuss.

   What literally do you see?

   How does the image change?

   What does this image say about this person?

5. Next, the sculptor and clay switch roles. Repeat steps one through four.

Variation: If students are uncomfortable touching each other, have the sculptor model exactly what they want physically while the clay mirrors them.

ACTIVITY: CREATE A FROZEN GROUP IMAGE In groups of four to six, create two images similar to the ideas stressed in the above exercise.

1. Create a group image of an enjoyable activity that a group of people would be involved in.

2. Create a group image of what happens to those people when that activity is taken away.

3. Show the two images together by starting with the first and moving to the second in an eight count.

4. Share and discuss the frozen images with the class.

Variation: Use the first image to describe the word *freedom* and the second image to describe *oppression* or *freedom taken away*.

WRAP UP Ask the students:

What do you need to survive?

How do you survive day to day in middle school?

When things get really bad, how do you keep your head up?

What do humans need to survive?

What is one thing that no one can take away from you?

Methodology

- role drama
- frozen images
- group discussion
- partner and group debate

Focus

How many people are at risk from a natural disaster and how would we rescue them?

Materials

- photos of natural disasters
- photos of World War II American and Russian soldiers freeing Holocaust victims

Student Objectives

- Discuss and create a natural disaster through creating frozen images.
- Define the different roles of a rescuer through role-play.
- Work as an ensemble in role to explore the fate of three families; state the consequences of their decisions.

Lesson and Content Structure

- Share pictures of natural disasters.
- Discuss as a class:

    What is a natural disaster?

    Why do people rebuild their homes and communities in the same place after those homes are destroyed?

    Who helps rebuild their community?

    Who rescues them?

    What qualities does a rescuer possess?

    How much are you willing to risk to save someone's life?

ACTIVITY: A DAY IN THE LIFE OF A NATURAL DISASTER   Break into groups of 4–5 students. Choose a natural disaster and create three frozen images to represent a day in the life of a community.

1. Beginning: What people were doing before the disaster?

2. Middle: The disaster hits.

3. End: After the disaster; picking up the pieces.

Discussion: Describe what you see. How is the community dealing with the aftermath?

ACTIVITY: TEACHER IN ROLE   The teacher is an editor of the big newspaper in town. She has called upon her fellow reporters (students) to interview the survivors of Hurricane George. She says, "Greetings fellow reporters! I'm so glad that all of you could make it today despite the nasty weather. As you know our town has been hit by one of the largest hurricanes this year. I understand there are many people who have lost their homes and maybe some who lost their lives. It is up to you to go find the survivors and get their story. Please be as sensitive as possible. This is a very fragile situation. Are there any questions?"

1. Break into teams of two.

2. Label each either A or B.

3. Person A is the reporter who interviews person B.

4. Person B shares their story of how they survived Hurricane George. Some questions to consider:

   Who rescued you?

   How did you hold on when things got really bad?

   What words of advice do you have for people who have never experienced a hurricane?

5. Switch places.

6. Person A is now a rescuer who tells their story of their rescue mission while person B interviews them.

ACTIVITY: TOWN MEETING: GROUP DECISION   We are all huddled in a group shelter together. We are past capacity and there is no room to lie down on the floor. Food is running out and the end of the storm is not in sight. There are three families who want to enter our already overcrowded shelter. What should we do?

1. Divide the students into pairs to argue the pros and cons of letting more people into the shelter.

2. As a group, discuss the consequences of letting three more families into the overcrowded shelter or leaving them out in the storm. What are the pros and cons? How do these weigh on our conscience?

Wrap-Up   Share photos of American and Russian soldiers and Danish citizens rescuing Jews from concentration camps. Consider:

What does it take to make a hero?

How are these rescue missions different or the same as saving someone from a natural disaster?

Step Two: Learning the Play

[Deb used a staged reading activity to introduce the play; the reading was then integrated with interactive drama work, as illustrated in the following lesson. Other methods she used to explore the scenes were teacher-in-role, discussion, role-play, frozen images, story as a springboard, library research, (questioning and inquiry), and student journal writing. Throughout the reading of the script, the students actively questioned the play, filling up a question box located in a visible spot in the classroom (Alexander 1999, 33).]

DRAMA LESSON

Topic

Act I.1: Otto Frank returns to the Annex for the first time since the end of the war. What memories does the Annex hold for Otto?

Methodology

- group discussion
- story telling
- journal writting

Materials

- personal item from home

Student Objectives

Design the Annex.

Lesson and Content Stucture

- Discuss how Otto Frank first discovers the Annex when he returns from the concentration camp.

    How do you show the personalities of people who might have lived there at one time?

    What do the walls look like?

What is on the floor?

What kind of furniture is there?

What is the condition of everything?

How do specific props represent character or story?

ACTIVITY: BRING IN A PERSONAL PROP   Students bring in an item from home that they think they might see lying on the Annex floor, and which Otto Frank might find. Create a demonstration for the students by bringing in four or five personal props of your own. Use an open space for your demonstration. Turn over a few pieces of furniture, such as a desk or a chair, and place your props in very specific areas in relation to the furniture. Once the props are placed, pick one prop up and tell a story from Otto Frank's point of view. For example, "I remember this pink sweater. I gave this to my wife for her birthday. I'm surprised she kept it this long. Oh look . . . there's a stain from where she spilled her coffee when Anne was chasing Peter around the table." Next, ask students one at a time, to place their props in the space and to tell their story. By the end of the exercise the classroom should be transformed into the Annex. Discuss as a class: What kind of memories does your prop bring back for Otto Frank?

WRAP-UP: JOURNAL WRITING   Write in your journal Otto's first thoughts when he discovers your personal prop.

Who did it belong to?

How was it used?

Why didn't the Nazis confiscate it?

Step Three: Questions and Research

[Deb offers an overview of her approach to research and dramaturgy.]

It should be stressed with the students that research is about asking questions and not necessarily finding all of the answers. If the play is well written, the issues are complex and there is rarely a simple solution to the characters' problems.

The hardest step of the research is already done for the students since . . . the students . . . [have been] filling up [the] question box . . . in the classroom as they read the play. Students select one question that intrigues them to start their research. . . . They use the library, computer, Internet access, and interviewing as their tools to find out more information.

Check out several books ahead of time relating to the topic from the public library to use as a resource in the classroom. . . . Specific websites are great starting points students can explore for further information. . . . Use alternative methods of research such as music, research collages, artwork, and interviews. (Alexander 1999, 59–60)

Create several workstations in the classroom, each requiring a different method of research. The teams can rotate among workstations as they begin their research. There should only be one team per workstation.

Workstation One: juvenile literature and children's books

Workstation Two: music from the time period

Workstation Three: artwork from the time period

Workstation Four: computer access

Workstation Five: interview center (how to create a simple interview)

Workstation Six: school library (periodicals and abstracts)

Workstation Seven: history books and world atlas

Workstation Eight: collage center

Have students create a historical time line on the bulletin board. Put the characters from the play in the time line to see how history affected the action of the play.

Step Four: Design

Exploration of design and technology serve as a powerful tool for students to address their questions about aspects of the play. The following two sample lessons are excerpts from a larger unit that considers scenic, sound, lighting, and costume elements for the play.

LESSON 1

Topic

Scenery: How do we create the world of the Annex?

Methodology

- design exercises
- group discussion

Materials

- classroom furniture
- paper
- rulers
- no. 2 pencils
- colored pencils

Student Objectives

- Transform the classroom into the world of the play by moving classroom (or rehearsal) furniture around.
- Place furniture in proscenium, thrust, and arena settings.
- Choose one character from the play and design their room with paper and pencil.

Lesson and Content Structure

- Give the students a variety of classroom or rehearsal furniture. Their task is to transform the classroom or a designated space into the world of the play. For example, create the four rooms in the Annex: Anne and Mr. Dussel's room, Van Daan's attic, Peter's room, and the main living area with a sink and stove.
- Discuss the following:

  What is missing?

  How do we personalize these rooms to show who occupies them?

  How do these rooms reflect the personality of the characters and the conflict of the play?

ACTIVITY: DIFFERENT THEATRICAL SPACES   How do we adapt this world we've created for the stage? First, discuss the three different kinds of stages:

proscenium: audience on one side

thrust: audience on three sides

arena: audience on four sides (in the round)

How would we adjust the set for each of these stages? What considerations do we have to make? Discuss the following:

sightlines

levels

planes

diagonals

stage pictures

audience

What furniture/set pieces can we do without? What kinds of props can we use to dress the set? Describe the walls. Where is the furniture onstage placed?

Lastly, students choose one of the configurations of the set either in proscenium, thrust, or arena. Based on what they designed, they draw a ground plan that they could give to the director for rehearsal purposes. Ask the students:

What do you need to inform the director about?

What challenges do you face with this set?

What are you willing to change? Why?

What do you want to stay the same? Why?

WRAP-UP Choose one character and design their room on paper. For example, how does Anne decorate her side of the room, as opposed to Mr. Dussel? How do their decorations reflect their personalities? Why is set dressing so important?

LESSON 2

Topic

Costuming: How do costumes help define character?

Methodology
- design activities
- group discussion

Materials
- 8–10 bags full of scraps
- 8–10 boxes of safety pins
- picture from the 1940s (male and female)
- paper
- colored pencils
- no. 2 pencils

Student Objectives
- Explore line, shape, and color through pinning different pieces of fabric to your clothing.
- Replicate a 1940s fashion with the bag of scraps and one model.
- Start to draw a costume rendering for a specific character from the play.

Lesson and Content Structure
1. Break students into groups of four or five.
2. Give each group a bag of scraps.
3. Have students explore the many different ways to drape their costume pieces; they can pin their scraps on any way they want.
4. See what each group comes up with and share.

ACTIVITY   Show students a picture of a costume from the time period of the play. Have them choose one person in their group to be the model and the other three the designers. Their task is to re-create the costume to the best of their abilities using their bag of scraps and safety pins. Girls and boys can work separately for the draping portion of this lesson. Discuss as a class: How does the placement of fabric on the body change the shape of the garment? What choices of fabric do you use to show character?

WRAP-UP   Each student must select one character from the play they are reading and create a costume rendering on paper. They can pin scraps of fabric to their rendering to show the color and texture of the costume. Discuss as a class: How do the costumes reflect that the characters have been hiding in the Annex for two years? How do the costumes change to reflect a passage of time? How do we show that the characters have lost weight?

Step Five: Create a Theatre Company

With the help of the teacher, students divide into three theatre companies and assign themselves to specific roles. The final class project/production consists of

- a dramaturgical display on a bulletin board
- a student resource packet
- a short performance by each company of one long scene or several shorter scenes.

The performances are shared with the school or selected classes.

ACTIVITY: WHICH ROLE BEST FITS YOU? JOINING A THEATRE COMPANY   A good theatre company is only as good as its members. Discuss how this project can be a team effort. Identify protocols and procedures for working together. Students read the Theatre Company Job Descriptions handout and answer the questions (see Figure 4–10, pages 130–31).

After the students are divided into three companies, they meet as a group with the teacher and check in with each other about their progress at least once a week. They make decisions together about how to help each other meet deadlines.

ACTIVITY: DRAMATURGICAL DISPLAY   The dramaturgs create a bulletin board to display all of the research the class has done in steps one through four of Model B. The intention is to help the audience better understand the play. The dramaturgy bulletin board should include, but is not limited to:

- historical facts
- historical time line
- design information

Figure 4–10 *Theatre Company Job Descriptions*

Please read the job descriptions and then answer the questions that follow to the best of your ability. Your opinion does matter. Take your time with your considerations. Feel free to discuss your thoughts with me.

JOB 1: The Director

Directors need to be leaders. They are responsible for helping create a unified vision for your scene. They must be able to work well with many people including the actors, designers, and technicians. They will stage and block a short scene, meet with the designers on a regular basis, and help create a ground plan for your scene. They will keep a director's book.

JOB 2: The Stage Manager

Stage managers must be extraordinarily organized. They must have excellent people skills because they are responsible for keeping the lines of communication open between the director, actors, designers, dramaturgs, and front of house. They are responsible for overseeing setup and strike at rehearsals every day. They will run the technical rehearsals and call the show during performance. They are responsible for overseeing props, sets, costumes, and other technical needs. They will keep a prompt book and help people who request specific information.

JOB 3 & 4: Actors

Actors must always be ready for rehearsals by warming up ahead of time and being on task. They will work closely with the director and stage manager. They are to help with technical duties when asked by the stage manager, and they are responsible for helping set up and strike after rehearsal.

JOB 5 & 6: Designers

Designers are responsible for designing the sets, costumes, lights, and sound. They will work closely with the director and stage manager to make sure the vision of the scene is realized. Designers will also work closely with the dramaturgs to let them know if there is any research material that they need so they can make a specific decision. They will be required to help build the technical elements and oversee crews during the process. Designers will be required to document their process by drawing renderings, building scale models, and justifying color choices.

JOB 7: Assistant Stage Managers (ASM)/Technical Support

ASMs will work directly with the stage manager. They are responsible for helping meet the director's and actors' needs. They will help with setup and strike for each rehearsal. When they are not needed in rehearsal, they will assist the designers, front of house, or dramaturgs depending on the need. They will work backstage for the performance.

Figure 4–10 (Continued)

JOB 8: Front Of House/Box Office/Marketing

This is a good position for students who excel in math and visual arts. Front of house/box office/marketing people are responsible for organizing the audience. They decide where the audience sits and they set up the seats. They will be responsible for overseeing the ushers on the day of performance. They are responsible for creating a ticketing system and deciding how to sell the tickets. They are also responsible for letting the school know about the performance through announcements, posters, flyers, and any other marketing techniques they want to use.

JOB 9 & 10: Dramaturgs

Dramaturgs need to be computer literate. They are responsible for setting up the dramaturgy board with specific information about the show. They should select the best work done by the students during our study of this play and be creative in how they display the work. They are also responsible for helping create the layout for the student resource packet and for collecting the program information to publish for the performance.

NOTE: Students with certain job titles (front of house/box office/marketing or dramaturg) work with all of the companies.

Questions

1. List your first, second, and third choices.

2. For each choice, answer the following questions:

   Why do you want this job?

   What strengths do you bring to this job?

   What role do you not want? Why?

- costume renderings
- scenic design
- photos from the process
- description of theatre company roles
- student responses about roles and process
- themes and issues

ACTIVITY: STUDENT RESOURCE PACKET   The student resource packet is a program that will be handed out to every audience member in order to prepare them for what they are about to see. The student resource packet is produced by the dramaturgs and is similar to the bulletin board except it is in the form of a small booklet. For this activity the emphasis is on layout versus writing. The student resource packet sums up steps one through four of Model B. Resource packets should include:

- table of contents
- names of everyone involved in the process and their roles
- background information (historical data)
- plot of the play
- themes and issues
- design page
- director's notes
- games and activities
- special thanks
- bibliography or where to get more information

ACTIVITY: PERFORMANCE OF SCENES The teacher selects one to three strong scenes from the script that involve two to three actors. Each scene is no longer than fifteen minutes (see Figure 4–11 for suggestions). Each company is responsible for directing, acting, and the production elements for their scene(s).

Figure 4–11 *Suggested Scenes from* **The Diary of Anne Frank**

In *The Diary of Anne Frank,* there aren't any two-person scenes that last very long, so each group can produce two to three scenes. I suggest using the following scenes:

Act I.2: Anne and Peter
Anne and Peter meet for the first time. Anne is admiring his cat Moushi.
Anne: "What's your cat's name?"

Act I.3: Mr. and Mrs. Van Daan
Mr. and Mrs. Van Daan are arguing about Mr. Van Daan's smoking habit.
Mr. Van Daan: "Isn't it bad enough here without your sprawling all over the place?"

Act I.3: Anne and Mr. Dussel
Anne and Mr. Dussel discover that they're sharing a room together.
Anne: "You're going to share my room with me."

Act II.1: Anne and Peter
Peter takes Anne her cake after she's had a fight with her family and abruptly leaves the room. This is the first time where Anne and Peter really have a conversation. They discover they are not as alone as they first thought they were.
Peter: "You left this."

Figure 4–11   (Continued)

Act II.2: Anne and Peter
Anne and Peter's first date
Anne: "Aren't they awful?"

Variation: Students can create their own scenes based on what isn't in the script to
help answer some of their questions about the characters. For example, one could
write a scene from Mrs. Frank's point of view about how she is unable to communicate with Anne. Or Mrs. Van Daan grilling Peter about his date up in the attic. Or
students can create their own modern-day version of *Anne Frank* by exploring a
parallel situation of what might be going on in the world, community, or school
right now.

The performance includes a brief description from each company of the process that they went through to get to this point. The post-show discussion is facilitated by a teacher or student. Reflections about the process take place through
group discussion, self-evaluation, and journal writing.

Ideas for Further Reflection

Taking Another Look at What Is

Ask yourself these questions about your current program:

- What is the relationship of my theatre curriculum and my program to that
  of the rest of the school?

- What is the balance of instruction, reflection, production, aesthetics,
  history, and criticism in my theatre program? What is the relationship
  between curricular and cocurricular activities? Does this balance offer
  comprehensive education in theatre?

- What is the relationship of my theatre curriculum and my program to that
  of the rest of the school?

Another Look at What Could Be

Let yourself imagine what is possible. Ask yourself:

- If the next time I went to my school I had a new, comprehensive theatre
  program, what would it look like? How is the whole program balanced
  and interconnected? What is my emphasis, and how do I allocate time and
  resources? What collegial relationships do I have?

- How does the content and practice in this program relate to content and practice in other art disciplines and other academic subjects students study?

- What challenges and obstacles were faced and overcome to bring about this change? Who helped me, and what resources and support did we garner in this process of change?

Another Look at What Will Be

What opportunities for change do the answers to the previous questions point to?

Notes

1. Discipline-Based Theatre Education was developed by Kim Wheetley for the Southeast Center for Education in the Arts (SCEA), a nationally recognized center for professional development located at the University of Tennessee at Chattanooga. SCEA was prompted in this move by the development of Discipline-Based Art Education (DBAE) initiated in 1985 by the Getty Center for Education in the Arts. DBAE is an effort to make art education more comprehensive and on equal footing with other academic subjects taught in schools. Believing that the arts are marginalized because of narrow focus on art production, DBAE advocates sought to expand art education through inclusion of aesthetics, art history, and art criticism. Inherent in all discipline-based initiatives are interactions between arts specialists and classroom teachers that foster study of other disciplines in arts classrooms and inclusion of the arts in other subjects.

2. There are a number of recent national projects and initiatives intended to foster and support arts integration and interdisciplinary arts education. For example, *The National Standards for Arts Education* (Consortium of National Arts Education Associations 1994) includes dance, music, theatre, and visual arts standards addressed at connections and relationships between art forms. In 2002, the Consortium of National Arts Education Associations published *Authentic Connections: Interdisciplinary Work in the Arts* to assist arts educators in teaching the arts with integrity through these national standards. The Interstate New Teacher Assessment and Support Consortium (INTASC), a program of the Council of Chief State School Officers, has developed *Model Standards for Licensing Classroom Teachers and Specialists in the Arts* (2002). This document presents principles "to clarify how the common core of teacher knowledge and skills play out for both classroom teachers and arts specialists in the context of teaching the arts" (2002). The Annenberg Foundation and the J. Paul Getty Trust have jointly initiated integrated arts education in schools through their Transforming Education Through the Arts Challenge. Arts for Academic Achievement is one Annenberg-funded initiative coordinated by the Minneapolis Public Schools and the Perpich Center. The Center for Applied Research and Educational Improvement at the University of

Minnesota is evaluating the initiative and publishing this information. The Annenberg/Corporation for Public Broadcasting (A/CPB) has developed a series of professional development videotapes and related websites. *The Arts in Every Classroom: A Workshop for Elementary Teachers* airs on the A/CPB Channel (www.learner.org). *Connecting with the Arts: A Teaching Practices Library* and *Workshop for Middle Grades Teachers* has been completed. *Instructional Practices in the Arts: A Workshop for High School Teachers* is in development.

3. Peer Assistance and Leadership, or PALs, is a national peer mentorship program that prepares high school students to work as mentors to elementary and middle school students.

5 *Theatre Education Outside the Box*

It seems clear to me that there is a deep connection between children and artists: They both want to discover the truth, to imagine the impossible, to delight in the now, and to name what is beautiful. As we listen to the news and struggle with our own families, careers, and communities, there is an urgent need for our children and our artists to take these journeys of discovery together.

—Abigail Adams, Director

In high school I was in theatre arts and did not have very good teachers. . . . I put myself in community theatre so that I could get a better experience and it truly changed my life. . . . I saw with my own eyes what theatre could do [for] those who love it.

—Rebecca Podsednik, Preservice Teacher

Embracing Community as Part of Professional Theatre

This book would not be complete without acknowledging that a lot of theatre education for secondary school students is taking place *outside* of school and traditional school structures. Professional theatres, youth theatres, community theatres, and a host of community-based agencies and organizations offer learning opportunities in theatre for large numbers of young people. Some students attend schools with no theatre programs; others turn to community-based programs as refugees fleeing theatre programs where their voices aren't heard or their presence noticed. They seek a place where they are welcomed and where they can find diverse, high-calibre theatre experiences. They find value working with artists who share their interests and passions and who appreciate their unique talents.

A recent interview with Peter Brosius, director of Children's Theatre Company (CTC), Minneapolis, highlights the theatre education role professional theatre organizations are playing as they reach out to "underserved" youth. CTC commissioned a play exploring tensions between African American and Somali immigrant children in the neighborhood around the theatre. They also produced *Antigone* using promenade style (no seats) so the actors could mingle with audience members—a soldier could push audience members aside, or "Creon might grab you and dance with you," said Brosius. He called their production of *Antigone* a "very vivid, muscular theatrical presentation" and noted that young people in the audience had "eyes as big as saucers." His challenge to adolescents: "You think you know what theatre is? We're going to surprise you" (Lamb 2003).

Professional artists can surprise, intrigue, and challenge adolescents in any number of ways. Allison Manville Metz (2002) wondered if watching and creating avant-garde theatre might be an engaging vehicle for self-expression for disenfranchised youth. She developed a project bringing together students from the public schools and artists at Salvage Vanguard, an avant-garde theatre in Austin.

> School doesn't teach me. It oppresses me.
> —High-school student, New York City

Metz raised a provocative question and suggested new avenues for theatre teacher-artists to explore.

> The importance of alternative education, as well as arts education, has been documented, but what about alternative arts education? Not only do I believe that avant-garde theatre has a lot to offer young people, I believe the world of avant-garde theatre has much to learn from youth on the margins of society. If theatre educators, artists, and marginalized youth can begin to appreciate the potential of a reciprocal relationship between the theatre form and the young population, there is no telling how the future of art and the future of young lives can be enhanced. (98)

For many of our nation's children, a touring production, a one-day residency with an artist, or a community theatre class will be the only theatre education they receive. The teaching artists I interviewed, however, recognize that plunking children into the seats of a theatre or leading one-day "drive-by dramas" is not theatre education and is far from best practice.

This chapter looks at artists and arts organizations that offer learner-centered and socially responsible theatre experiences to middle and high school students. Whether in their own venues or through partnerships with schools, artists who embrace principles of best practice provide rich perspectives about theatre and theatre making. The artists profiled in this chapter see their mission as serving all members of the community, young, old, and in between. They offer a glimpse of a broad range of forward-looking practice and activity.

People's Light and Theatre Company

Artists in the resident, professional company at People's Light and Theatre (PLT) are actively engaged in the life of Malvern, Pennsylvania, and its surrounding communities. On a visit to the theatre, forty-five minutes from Philadelphia, I was struck by the easy place young people occupy in many of the activities of this theatre organization. To artistic director Abigail Adams (2002), the connection to young people and the community is one of PLT's core values. It means "being engaged in the community—living here, being a soccer coach as well as an actor . . . so . . . you're not removed from the community." Abbey talked with me about why she chooses to work with young people in her professional practice.

> I work with kids because I like to be in their company. . . . And I think that makes it a genuine experience and . . . a more equitable power structure. . . . Yes, it's a led collaboration, but there are times . . . with all of us who deal with kids . . . where the adults are in a collegial setup with the kids. . . . Everything I do with the kids is reflected in everything I do with the resident company or the national circle of artists that we're working with. There's absolutely no difference to me in what I'm learning or working on. (2002)

PLT makes long-term commitments to area children. Years ago they began New Voices, a program for young people from Chester, a city with struggling schools and a depressed economy about forty-five miles from PLT. PLT realized that if these children were going to come to the theatre in Malvern, they were going to have to provide transportation—so PLT got a van. PLT teaching artists eat meals with the kids, teach them, act in season productions with them, and help them with their homework and college applications. The first New Voices group began as sixth graders, and PLT staff worked with them until most graduated from high school. It wasn't easy in the early years, but ultimately New Voices became a rich learning experience for all involved. Some members of this original group now work at the theatre, and staff have begun working with the third New Voices group.

Another PLT program is the Teen Ensemble. I watched an artful process in which two resident artists guided the group through improvisation as a way of introducing *Lysistrata*, the play they were going to perform. In Ensemble members discussed male and female stereotypes, enacted these physically, and then switched roles so boys could experiment with hyperfemale characterizations and vice versa. Reflections and thoughtful criticism flowed easily in the group. They went on to create scenes parallel to events in the play and also talked about scenic, historical, and aesthetic issues. The overall goal of this work is for Teen Ensemble members "to ask themselves as creative and political human beings: 'What do I have to say?' and 'How do I best say it?'" (Peterson, K. 2002)

In addition to participating in New Voices and Teen Ensemble, students perform their own works and act in mainstage productions with resident company members. PLT teaching artists offer classes through their Project Discovery arts education program. The theatre's resident playwright, Russell Davis, also teaches as an artist-in-residence in local schools. PLT also offers the Theatre School, classes for adults and youth, and a process-oriented summer program, Summerstage. PLT teaching artists also work with the Young Women's Ensemble. Ensemble members investigate gender identities, stereotypes, and how theatre can amplify the voices of girls. (See page 151 for sample lesson plans addressing these topics.)

PLT is a living, breathing organism, responsive and connected to the world beyond the theatre's parking lot. They are neighbors and fellow citizens, partners who continue to grow, change, and serve young people with innovation and impact.

Stage One

Stage One is a professional theatre for young audiences in Louisville, Kentucky. They offer a range of educational programs as well as a broad season of plays for young and family audiences. I was a guest artist with Stage One and acted in their production of *The Music Lesson* by Tammy Ryan (2000). This experience allowed me to see the breadth of Stage One's commitment to theatre education.

In each season, Stage One includes provocative new works that challenge stereotypical expectations of theatre for young people. For *The Music Lesson*, Ryan worked closely with artistic director J. Daniel Herring to uncover the provocative and timely themes brought to life by both adult and adolescent characters (Herring 2002). The play is set in the United States and moves backward and forward in time and place. It presents the impact of the siege in Sarejevo on two Bosnian refugees—gifted music teachers—and their Bosnian students. Flashbacks to the war period unfold in counterpoint to interactions with two American students who are facing the aftermath of a different war—their parent's divorce. *The Music Lesson* explores the healing influence of music, the life and joy that can come after great loss, and the ennobling roles of both teacher and student.

In addition to producing interesting new theatre pieces, J. Daniel is committed to offering young people theatre experiences that challenge them to reconsider their views of themselves and the world. He believes students need a comprehensive theatre education that includes seeing high-quality professional theatre and working directly with professional artists.

> I don't really believe in . . . a situation where a high school becomes insular and . . . the only experience that those . . . young people have is at that high school. I don't care if it's a performing arts school, I don't care if it's a magnet school. . . . If that's the only experience they're having, it isn't a complete arts education. . . . It's just like [if] you teach visual art in a school without ever seeing the masters' works. . . . I think you have to see Picasso's work, and you have to see Van Gogh's work. I think you have to see Shakespeare's work. You have to see Tennessee Williams' work. I think you have to see Suzan Zeder's work [and] . . . James Still's work . . . Tammy Ryan's work . . . if you are . . . teaching [young] people. . . . Students need to see . . . artists making art. (Herring 2002)

Associate artistic director Steven Jones talks about his view of comprehensive theatre education and Stage One's approach to the balance between seeing theatre and learning about theatre.

> [For children] it's the aesthetic experience . . . of going to the theatre and being a part of . . . the art on stage, but . . . it's also . . . being in a classroom where drama is the

teaching tool, [where] drama is the instructional strategy so you get the whole process part . . . too.

At Stage One . . . I think we're becoming one of the models . . . where there is equality between the two—where what's happening on the stage is so intrinsically connected to what's happening in the classroom that one doesn't, can't, happen alone. (2002)

Stage One staff build bridges between children in the community and their work at the theatre. Teaching artists, including J. Daniel, teach at area schools and for the Stage One Summer Theatrefest program. They prepare study guides showing correlations between the productions and the Kentucky core content in drama, the instructional requirements of the Kentucky Education Reform Act.

Students in Kentucky are assessed at the fifth-, eighth-, and eleventh-grade levels in . . . the drama core content. What's interesting though, is there's currently no way for teachers in Kentucky to get theatre certification. So we as an organization [have responded]. (Jones 2002)

The theatre now employs experienced teaching artists who teach the drama core content in area schools through residencies.

There aren't [theatre] teachers out there [to teach in the schools]. I had to turn [classroom] teachers away this year because I did not have the staff. . . . Teachers [were] calling me up saying "Steven, I need somebody to come in and teach this drama core content. I need you to come in and tell my kids about the role of the actor, the role of the director, the role of the production designer, the role of the playwright because in a few weeks they're about to be tested on it, and I don't know enough about it to do it." (Jones 2002)

To address the shortage of qualified drama and theatre teachers, Steven formed a partnership with a local college. Adapting a program he developed while working with Dan Kelin at Honolulu Theatre for Youth, he teaches drama classes for education majors at the college. He then mentors them as they implement their college work with children in the schools (Jones 2002; Kelin 2001).

Believing Stage One has a bigger role to play in their community, Steven, and education director Andrew Harris, received a grant from the state of Kentucky for Inner Visions, a theatre education program for the State Agency Children's Program schools. The young people in these schools have faced many troubles and challenges in their lives and are often held in their schools in "lockdown."

I think that these populations of kids benefit the most from being exposed to the arts. . . . I've watched their eyes be opened and their hearts and minds . . . rocked when they see possibilities for themselves in the arts as artists. . . . They connect to these very tactile, get up on your feet, and "let me reach deep down in my soul and tell you what it is that I'm feeling" sort of experiences. [If you] look at artists in the field who have received critical acclaim both on stage and in films and you start digging around in their pasts . . . you find out [some of] these kids were hellions.

I think in traditional settings these kids get marginalized and they get pushed to the sides, and our education system isn't arranged so that everybody can be accommodated. . . . There's a part of me that believes we're all artists. . . . I want to turn these kids on to the artists within themselves because this is their way out. This is where they're going to find solace, and this is where they're going to find success. I've watched it happen over and over. (Jones 2002)

Steven sees even more room for partnerships between Stage One and local secondary schools.

I've just recently . . . gotten back into . . . directing secondary [school] kids [as a freelance artist]. . . . I told J. Daniel, "You know what, we've got an opportunity here to pair these kids up with . . . some professionals in our organization. . . . Do you have any problem—if I'm paying these folks on a freelance basis—with me utilizing them?" And he said "Absolutely not." So our technical director at Stage One became the technical director for me in my productions and worked with the students to build the set, and . . . not only build the sets but . . . he gave the design responsibilities to them. . . . He mentored them in designing the set and then they came [to] the Stage One shop and built the set.

Stage One could afford to adopt a few [secondary school] theatre departments in this city and say "You know . . . we don't have money to commit to you . . . but we're going to commit to sharing our knowledge. And we're going to open our shop doors, and . . . you can come backstage, and we're going to have three or four talkbacks with [our] directors." We can afford to do that. (Jones 2002)

Flint Youth Theatre

Flint, Michigan is the birthplace of General Motors and the United Auto Workers. Since the 1970s when the American automotive empire began to falter, Flint's economy has steadily declined, and its unemployment rate has soared to twice the national average. Flint is also the home of the Flint Youth Theatre (FYT). This nationally recognized program has long offered innovative and diverse programming in partnership with the Flint schools and cultural and civic groups. In addition to a season of their own productions, FYT offers year-round classes, hosts professional touring productions for young audiences, and explores and develops new work with and for young people and adults to bring about social change. They have devised original pieces dealing with violence, growing up female, and displaced persons.

One FYT project in particular, which united the community against school violence, illustrates how the practice of theatre education at a professional theatre continues to evolve in service to young people and their community (Lazarus 2001).

THEATRE AS CIVIC DIALOGUE

For more than half a century, interspersed with a season of fairy tales and traditional and contemporary plays for family audiences, FYT artists have produced works with youth and adult performers that shed light on controversial issues important to their community. Artistic director Bill Ward joined FYT in the late

1980s and brought with him a new aesthetic and a desire to push the boundaries for FYT artistically. Sue Wood, who was then FYT's executive director, agreed that the theatre should challenge the community to think in new ways about itself and about theatre for and with young people.

As history unfolded in Flint, it became clear to both Sue Wood (2001) and Bill Ward (2001a) that FYT's mission to produce challenging theatre of the highest quality would best be served by a close and active relationship with the Flint community and with the Flint public schools. In a 1995 study by the Flint schools, it was determined that Flint ninth graders were 70 percent more likely to have engaged in group fighting at school than the national norm and 400 percent more likely to have used a gun or other weapon to get something from a person (Flint Youth Theatre 2001, 52). After the shootings at Columbine High School, Flint area schools reported a rash of bomb scares, gun threats, and gang attacks in elementary, middle, and high schools. Flint was thrown into the national spotlight when five-year-old Kayla Rolland was fatally shot by a classmate at her school (2001). Bill reflects that

> suddenly Columbine is here. . . . It's not just something happening over there and something I'm just responding to because I've seen it televised. I am here in it. . . . [Our] work is an attempt . . . to respond to that particular incident and all the other incidents like it. (Ward 2001a)

Bill's response to school violence in Flint took shape through a special project focused at stimulating civic dialogue and uniting the community against school violence. FYT's project was selected as one of sixteen in the country to be supported by the Animating Democracy Lab component of the Animating Democracy Initiative (ADI). ADI was coordinated by Americans for the Arts and funded by the Ford Foundation. Pam Korza, speaking for Americans for the Arts (2001a), said "We have observed that the arts can play a role by providing a compelling and alternative point of entry and by serving as convener, offering safe places for difficult dialogue."

For the FYT lab project, Sue enlisted the support and active participation of a range of Flint community and grassroots partners. In conjunction with FYT's drama work exploring school violence, each partner organized activities designed to stimulate civic dialogue: study circles, a university symposium, a mini-grant program for schools and community organizations, a student conference, and a video documentary of the project.

The centerpiece of the FYT lab project was an original performance piece entitled . . . *My Soul to Take,* created by Bill. The production itself represented public discourse as it confronted, surprised, and challenged school and public audiences to think critically about and discuss this complex issue. In an interlacing of light, sound, movement, music, and language, FYT artists captured the swirl of opinions surrounding a school shooting. More than a play, this multilayered performance collage juxtaposed time and space and was deliberately nonprescriptive as it shed light on the multiple and conflicting issues influencing school shootings. The easy rhetoric of politicians and the pleas of parents were heard as causes were sought and blame placed. A chorus of plaintive voices asked what all in the audience were thinking: "Can't somebody do something?" We met the mother of a slain child in a moving series of monologues, each of which began, " . . . After the shooting, it seemed like there was always someone from the media coming up to me and asking me 'how it felt.'" We first learned about her son as a youngster full of love and imagination and later as a precocious, increasingly private adolescent filled with a passion for music. It was only toward the end of this eclectic montage that we again saw the mother and realized her son was not a victim of the shooting, but the shooter himself, a victim of another kind of violence. And all the while, ever-present and just left of center stage, stood a high-powered rifle propped vertically in a tall Plexiglas case. Audiences had come to ignore its presence, only to be haunted by their indifference by the play's conclusion.

Figure 5–1 . . . **My Soul To Take** *flier*

In the spirit of shared ownership, the piece began not with Bill as playwright alone at his computer, but with him as an observer to children's and community members' explorations of school violence through drama. In October 2000, British theatre artist and teacher Gillian Eaton led a series of process drama sessions with Flint's middle and high school students (Eaton 2001). As Bill observed these sessions from the side of the room, students improvised and discussed artwork, stories, and events that would reveal their feelings about rage, fear, and its impact on them. Groups of adults also participated with Eaton in process drama sessions in which they created improvisations and explored the Pied Piper story and the issue of "lost" children. Inspired by the work facilitated by Gillian, Bill wove a stylized version of the Pied Piper through . . . *My Soul to Take* and so presented a timeless metaphor of a piper who lures children away after government leaders fail to keep their promises. Based in the authentic perceptions of the Flint children and the adults who participated in the process drama sessions, the parallels of the story to today's society were profound. From these improvisations, his imagination, and extensive dialogue with Eaton as ad hoc dramaturg, Bill created . . . *My Soul to Take*.

After seeing the production, selected school groups participated in workshops with Eaton in which they used drama to talk about the play and the issues it raised for them. Four thousand people saw . . . *My Soul to Take*. It was estimated that more than four hundred students and adults participated in process drama sessions before and after the performances. More than thirteen hundred people participated in study circles, a community symposium, or a student conference organized by FYT as part of the project.

Bill admits there is a great deal to be gained artistically from theatre work of this kind. But there are also questions. He wonders if the art gets lost or if theatre colleagues would even view the work as art. Does the theatre piece become so inseparable from the issue that the work can't stand as a piece of art? How does issue-based theatre incorporate actual community and historical events into the work without exploiting either the issue or the victims or creating the perception that we are dwelling on an unpleasant event or issue?

And what about the children involved in the piece itself as well as in the audience? What preparation, follow-through, and follow-up is necessary to support inquiry, reflection, and age-appropriate participation? Who must partner with arts organizations like FYT to care for the needs of children when doing material of this kind and when working with adult performers who may be better able to process the information?

This work doesn't offer any kind of prescriptions. It doesn't pretend to do that. But it . . . serves as a way to illuminate issues and to cause people to think. . . . Maybe the work actually causes people to either have dialogue, or in the most wonderful of cases, causes people to become activists themselves and do something in their community.

—*Bill Ward*

OTHER CONSIDERATIONS

FYT's lab project serves as an example of the interlacing questions, concerns, rewards, and risks facing any arts organization doing socially responsible theatre work with and for young people. The work at FYT has been successful in large part because Bill and Sue share common concerns about their community and its children. They choose to be an active partner with the schools and other agencies willing to address community concerns. These factors cannot be underestimated as one considers the challenges and rewards of working with young people in socially engaged theatre projects (Lazarus 2001).

Creative Arts Team

Since the work of the Creative Arts Team (CAT) began in the 1970s, this professional theatre has exploded the boundaries of theatre education. Drawing on models of theatre-in-education (TIE) and other interactive theatre forms, CAT teaching artists work in classrooms and with parents, community leaders, and policy makers to confront issues facing New York City's young people. Their work is learner-centered and consciously socially engaged and socially responsible.

In the years since CAT began offering its own brand of theatre education, it has emerged as an international pioneer, disrupting assumptions about both the quality and the nature of theatre work with and for youth. CAT's professional teaching artists work in schools and community sites, engaging participants and facilitating their examination of social issues such as intimate relationship violence, teen pregnancy, parent-child relationships, gun violence, and violation of civil liberties. CAT teaching artists work with organizations around the world, from South Africa where they teamed with universities developing an AIDS outreach project for adolescents, to the Middle East where they worked with actors from different countries to create a piece for young people about tolerance.

Artistic director Chris Vine regularly interrogates CAT's pedagogy and methodologies. He spoke about working with CAT teaching artists to critically examine their own theatre techniques and practice.

> "Student-centered" [is] a phrase that everybody uses, but what does it actually mean in terms of the relationship between you the artist, the selection of the material that *you're* making, the curriculum students are having, [which is] cooked up [by the] schools, [and] the methodology . . . we use which we say . . . powers them, gives them voice. . . . ? And what are we trying to be student centered about and for? How do we recognize it is happening?
>
> [At CAT] we deal with social issues, but . . . [we do so] when the young people decide that they want to put them in their work or they come up with an issue [they've] discussed in their group. [Issues are] not coming in because I'm bringing in a curricular list saying, "All right, we're going to look at race for the moment or we're going to look at violence or we're going to look at whatever." (2000)

With the help of the Paul A. Kaplan Center, CAT is now able to offer professional development classes to new generations of teaching artists. One of their classes focuses on the CAT Youth Theatre program. Teachers and artists enrolled in this class are able to investigate the theory and practices Chris and Youth Theatre program director Helen White use to devise high-quality theatre with high-school students.

Teen members of the Youth Theatre program come from the different boroughs of New York. Throughout the year, the adolescents meet with Helen, Chris, and CAT teaching artists to make theatre as a community of artists.

> The CAT Youth Theatre does not begin with a list of extant objectives: there is no agenda of theatre skills to be taught, nor a list of social issues to be addressed, nor developmental outcomes to be achieved. The starting point is the young people themselves and an agreement to work in the medium of theatre. (White and Vine 2001, 9)

Youth and adults negotiate shared understandings about how they will work together as colearners and human beings. Exploring multifaceted topics and themes offered by the young people, company members devise and craft original productions.

Helen White talked about why she chooses to work in youth theatre.

> I think . . . youth theatre . . . brought together all the things I love most passionately in [the] most . . . satisfying way. . . . We create original theatre—the quality of the theatre has become increasingly higher and higher and higher. We're creating community with the young people that keeps expanding as the youth theatre has a longer [and] longer history. . . . And also . . . I've got Youth Theatre members who . . . [want] some support and some . . . ideas for how they're going [to start] their own youth theatres. So the work is . . . fulfilling and that community [keeps growing]. (2000)

Nurtured by their shared passion for theatre, artists of all ages are helping the Creative Arts Team continue its impressive growth.

Teaching Artists and Artists in Residence

> *At one point I was doing [some work as a professional playwright] and . . . I had to be away [from my middle school] for several days. . . . [When I came back the students] were wondering, "Well, why don't you just do that? . . . . You should be doing something else than just teaching . . . because you [can] do something else." I said, "Why not have the . . . strong artist in a teaching position? . . . [Playwrighting] is the something else that I do. [Teaching] is what I do.*
> —Gloria Bond Clunie, Teacher and Playwright

In parts of this country, many schools hire local artists to direct plays with high school or middle school students. This can sometimes be problematic for the youth involved. If the director-for-hire does not know the students, their needs, or their interests, students can be caught in awkward hierarchical or dogmatic interactions. If the director is not informed about learner-centered, socially responsible, and discipline-based practices, what are the students learning about the art and craft of theatre?

There are, fortunately, many wonderful exceptions. Independent freelance artists committed to principles of best practice can have a significant impact on the lives of young people. Susan diRende is one example. Working with Susan on several projects in recent years, I have found her approach to artmaking with young people inspiring and in keeping with the practices of many of the teachers interviewed for this book.

Susan is a Renaissance woman. She is a playwright, screenwriter, performer, movement artist, vocal coach, and director currently living in Los Angeles. Susan also has a palpable love of teaching. She has worked with high-school students in community-based programs and directed a number of shows at the high-school level. She nurtures students, challenges them, and fosters in them a conviction in their ability to make aesthetically pleasing theatre together (diRende 2002). She draws her inspiration from many sources.

> Otto Rank wrote once, "You cannot go to school to be an artist, you can only go to school as an artist." Whenever I work, whether with professionals or beginners, I am always clear that we are all equally artists. All I may have is greater skill or more knowledge, but we can only make art if we are all artists.
>
> For me one of the challenges . . . [is] to encapsulate the essence of fostering artistry into a process [for] . . . people who have little contact or experience with theatre.
>
> I heard someone define humans as meaning-making machines . . . and I do believe that each act of theatre is an act of making meaning. . . . Once humans collaborate and perform together in front [of] others, they create a communal experience of value and meaning, the impact of which lingers and expands through the culture. Each act of theatre is a breath in the life of human culture. How important is one breath to life?
>
> I also think theatre fosters understanding of difference. To effectively write or portray a character, you have to get inside their head, to come to terms with the good and bad in a range of types with a host of life experiences and perspectives. . . . And difference becomes attenuated by realizing how alike people's motives, fear, and dreams can be. . . . And this is not in the name of some abstract philosophy of compassion and tolerance but the visceral experience of identifying with a character.
>
> I had . . . students who struggled a whole semester with the idea of objectives in acting—that the character's actions are guided by what he or she wants from the other characters. It seemed they resisted knowing this about the characters in the play because they resisted knowing this about themselves. Then I realized their education had . . . [separated] them from a true knowledge of their desires, their wishes, their goals. The education system in the United States, it has been written, was designed to develop 10 percent leaders, 15 percent bourgeoisie, and the rest as laborers. I don't know how true that is, but . . . some relation to their own motivations had been stripped from them. . . . If alienation from the knowledge of one's motivations can produce followers, then it seems reconnecting people with their ability to see [their motivations] strikes me as a first step to developing leaders. (diRende 1996)

Each act of theatre is a breath in the life of human culture. How important is one breath to life?

—*Susan diRende*

Figure 5–2 *Teaching artists enliven students' understanding of theatre.*

Partnerships for Theatre Education

Many secondary school theatre educators build partnerships bridging schools to theatres, community centers, museums, universities, or other agencies and organizations. The result is a rich collaboration for the artists, teachers, and young people involved. Following are examples of several different kinds of partnerships.

Galumph Theatre

Galumph Theatre is an innovative, professional theatre company that draws on physical theatre styles, puppetry, masks, and interactive structures to involve audiences in imaginative ways. Chris Griffith is a producing artist with the company and also works as an independent artist in the Minneapolis area. He and Galumph bring their skills to partnerships with area schools. For one partnership, teaching artists spent most of a semester with "a class of students with cerebral palsy, Down's syndrome, and a variety of other physical and mental disabilities" (Griffith 2002a). One of the goals was for the students with special needs to find and share their voices because special needs [students] tend to be in their own little corner of the school, and no one else talks to them. . . . [During this residency] the students created puppet shows about their experiences as teenagers trying to fit in mainstream classes. (2002a)

These teens worked with about forty students in a studio art class to develop and build the props and puppets for the show.

Galumph teaching artists work in an interdisciplinary fashion, weaving content from across the curriculum into their residencies. They are also asked to be partners in the schools because of their reputation as a socially engaged theatre company.

> We'll often be asked to come into an inner city school and work with students who have very difficult times relating to each other. . . . There's a school [trying] to address the dropout rate . . . where . . . [we've worked with] . . . students. [The school has] us . . . work with [the Native American students] to create trust and to create a kind of base that they can build on for the rest of the year. . . . One of the things that happens . . . is that the students really learn how to take care of each other [and] learn how to be taken care of. (Griffith 2002a)

Cedar Falls City Youth Theatre

Gretta Berghammer has developed a different model of theatre education partnership. Gretta is a theatre professor at the University of Northern Iowa (UNI). She started a youth theatre by forming a partnership between the UNI theatre department, the community theatre, and the local arts center. The youth theatre now provides young people an opportunity to grow as artists and individuals. They work with university students, take classes, and create theatre productions. Gretta has created a developmentally sensitive, learner-centered program. For example, she feels strongly that the youth should self-cast for roles in productions. "Young people know better than I know when they're ready to [perform]. The students . . . ought to have control over how much risk they're taking in theatre [work]" (Berghammer 2002).

Gretta also talked about her socially responsible practice, equitable access to production experiences, and how a traditional approach to casting can create barriers to access.

> There is no model like that . . . in music and visual art. They . . . give kids instruments here in the fourth grade. . . . They try to match the instrument to the size of the child and what they're physically capable of doing. But whether [the students are] good or bad, they're playing in the orchestra. Same thing with art. . . . You don't not go to art class because you can't draw. And to me it [should be] the same philosophy [in theatre instead of] "You can't be in the play because you can't act." Well, how are you going to learn if you [are] a twelve-year-old? . . . Where do they get the experience? (Berghammer 2002)

Gretta is clear that it is her responsibility "to make . . . the best artful [production]" but she also ponders, "Whose standard of artistry are we holding these kids up to?"

Lincoln Community Playhouse

Another model arts organizations use to deliver direct theatre instruction to students is a partnership with a school or school district. The Lincoln Community Playhouse hosts a class, Advanced Theatre Company, for students in all of the Lincoln, Nebraska, high schools. The class is taught at the theatre by an experienced teaching artist. The class is held during the school day, which enables them to continue participating in their own school's cocurricular theatre program. The districtwide class builds on and extends learning opportunities not available in students' home schools.

Illusion Theatre

John Heinemann teaches in one of the Lincoln, Nebraska, high schools. He talks about another citywide partnership offered jointly by the State Health Department, the school district, and Illusion Theatre of Minneapolis. Illusion is a professional organization that devises and performs theatre pieces to stimulate dialogue, reflection, and action. They have developed a number of pieces including *TOUCH*, which is a collection of vignettes written about physical abuse for young audiences. Illusion has a program for high school students called TRUST: Teaching and Reaching Using Students of Theatre, which John coordinates for students in his school district. The high-school students produce Illusion scripts and tour to schools around the distrct.

> We want to bring art to children in its full-strength formulas: robust, powerful, idiosyncratic, critical, and more than a little bit dangerous. If we have to leave these attributes outside the classroom door, we would do better to leave art out of the curriculum altogether.
> —*Zemelman, Daniels, and Hyde*

> The school contributed by giving [me] two periods to work with a small number of kids. . . . The district pays a stipend [for a] community member who does the Health and Human Services aspect of performances and moderates [the] shows.
>
> We're doing so much more educating outside of the classroom. It's been an amazing, powerful tool, not only for the students who we perform for . . . but . . . [it's] an incredible experience for the actors. . . . It changes your life when a ten-year-old child comes up to you and says, "My mom's boyfriend does that to me, and I don't like it, and I want it to stop." . . . This high-school student has the power to get them to a [professional who will find a] place where they're safe and real change can happen. (Heinemann 2002)

The examples throughout this chapter illustrate the potential for theatre artists and educators to be colearners and coteachers of our young people. As secondary school teachers and professional community-based artists work and learn together, the box of twentieth-century theatre education will be recycled, discarded, or rebuilt.

An Example of Best Practice Theatre Education Outside the Box

Empowering Ophelia by Gillian McNally

Gillian McNally is a professional actor, director, and teaching artist currently working with People's Light and Theatre Company. While completing her MFA, she formed the Ophelia Project Ensemble and led the group as a teacher-director. The Ensemble of middle school girls developed an original adaptation of *The Light Princess* (MacDonald 1969). Named for *Reviving Ophelia* (Pipher 1994), the Ophelia Project Ensemble's goal was "to create a safe place where lost adolescent female voices could be heard" (McNally 2002a, 5). The following rehearsal plan is part of a learner-centered rehearsal process in which the girls share their voices and deconstruct assumptions about gender (McNally 2002b).

LESSON PLAN: OPHELIA PROJECT ENSEMBLE

Topic

- Devising *The Light Princess*

Focus

Gender

Materials

- large piece of paper
- marker

Teacher Objectives

- Create a sense of safety in playing characters of the opposite gender.
- Discuss and examine the girls' perspectives on female gender roles.
- Generate interesting material for the script of *The Light Princess*.

Student Objectives

- Engage in two activities to help focus energy.
- Discuss perceptions of gender characteristics.
- Physically enact the agreed-upon gender characteristics.
- Apply discussion of gender to three scenes from *The Light Princess*.

ACTIVITIY: WARM UP

What's on top of your pile?

1. Find a partner that is not in the same grade as you. Sit across from them.

2. Decide roles: One partner is A one is B.

3. "As, talk to partner B about your day for two minutes nonstop. Talk about things that could keep you from focusing on our work today." (Sidecoaching: Keep talking! Go further into detail about one particular event.)

4. Reverse roles.

Zip, Zap, Zop

1. Stand in a circle.

2. Everyone say "Zip, Zap, Zop." (Repeat four or five times.)

3. First person starts with the word "Zip." As they say the word, they point to another person across the circle, paying special attention to making eye contact with that person.

4. This person says the word "Zap" and points to a third person.

5. Third person passes "Zop" to a fourth person.

6. Fourth person starts the series again by passing "Zip."

7. Keep the cycle going. Once members get the rhythm of the game, encourage them to go faster.

ACTIVITY: SKILL OF THE DAY   As you know, each day we explore a different skill to add to our creation of *The Light Princess*. Since we have roles like the King and the Prince in *The Light Princess*, many of you will need to play male characters. We're going to look at how we view and represent masculine and feminine behaviors.

Gender Continuum Exercise*

1. On a large piece of paper, draw a line across it with *one* at the left end, *five* in the middle, and *ten* on the right end of the line. One is hypermasculine, ten hyperfeminine, according to stereotypes.

2. Decide who students know or think is a representative of *ten, one*, and *five*. (Make lists.) What are the behaviors of each category? Why do their choices fit these categories? For example, where does Michael Jackson

---

*Adapted from an exercise developed by Professor Stacy Wolf, the University of Texas at Austin.

belong and why? Gay men and gay women? Suggest other names for their consideration.

3. Have students walk around as themselves. Ask them to think about what number they are, but not to say it out loud.

4. Ask them to go to *one*. Sidecoach them to go further as *one*: "You're only at a *three*! Push yourself to go to a *one*—get extreme!"

5. Go to *ten*. Keep sidecoaching. Dare them to over exaggerate.

6. Have them do various activities in different number types, such as sitting/ standing and posing for a photographer.

Questions: Describe your experience during this exercise. Which did you feel most comfortable doing and why? What did you notice about how the group acted in the *one* versus the *ten*? Why do you think this is?

Scene Work

1. Break students into three groups.

2. Assign scenes five, six, and seven from the story *The Light Princess*.

3. Ask students to choose roles, decide what their "gender number" is for their character, and to be prepared to improvise their scene in ten minutes.

Share Scenes

1. Each group shares their prepared scene.

2. Ask those not in the scene, "What number do you think _____ was playing?" Ask actor if we are correct.

3. Redo scenes, asking the actors to change their "gender number."

4. Ask those watching, "How did the number changing alter their performance? How did it change the scene? Any ideas on how we could incorporate this into our play?"

ACTIVITY: CLOSING   Sit in a circle. One by one, go around the circle and say a short phrase that comes to mind about the rehearsal today.

Ideas for Further Reflection

Explore Partnerships

Take an inventory of potential partners in your community and how many you know or are in contact with on a regular basis. Initiate conversations about ways in which you could work together for children in your community.

Go to the Theatre

Seek out theatre organizations in your community whose work you admire or have never seen. Attend a representative sampling of their work, including classes, workshops, and residencies. What can you learn from them about the craft of theatre making, relationships with the community, or new play development? What about their work might be of value to your students? Invite friends and colleagues who may be unfamiliar with theatre to go with you. Generate dialogue about the works you see. Invite local artists to your program and discuss possible partnerships.

6

Breaking the Mold
Implications of Best Practice

> The students watch us, all the time. We must honestly ponder what they see, and what we want them to learn from it.
>
> —THEODORE AND NANCY SIZER

Implications of Best Practice for the Field

The notion of best practice raises many questions and serves as a call to action for our field. Teachers and artists I spoke with talked about steps that must be taken on a number of fronts—by teachers, artists, administrators, and policy makers—to ensure a meaningful future for secondary school theatre education. Following are steps most frequently suggested as catalysts for change at the local, state, and national levels.

- Develop opportunities through school districts and professional associations to see multiple versions of best practice in action, to observe and interact with colleagues in classrooms and rehearsals, and to participate in mentorship programs and exchanges.
- Generate dialogue—pursue and strengthen partnerships among educators, artists, university theatre faculty, education faculty, and leaders in government, civic, and cultural agencies and organizations at the local, state, regional, and national levels.
- Create opportunities for critical analysis of our work.
- Conduct research about comprehensive, learner-centered, socially responsible secondary school theatre education and publish findings broadly.
- Engage in advocacy within and outside of our field at the grassroots and national levels.

Rethinking Theatre Teacher Education

The most obvious action needed, however, is the revision of theatre teacher education to better correlate with best practice principles. In the remainder of this chapter, university and college professors share ways they are teaching and modeling these principles with their preservice teachers.

Forty years from now many of today's theatre education majors will still be teaching in our schools. During that time the tides of social and political change will wash over those schools continually, removing traces of today's reform efforts and leaving new landmarks, new buzzwords and trends, newly revised standards and curricula, and reconfigured requirements. What are the tools necessary for a novice teacher to prepare for a voyage of this kind?

To help teachers navigate the currents and eddies of these changes, to respond to the challenges they will face, to teach and to reach all of the children they will encounter, there must be shifts in the way teachers are educated. New theatre teachers themselves must have a comprehensive theatre education, one that seeks connections among ideas, methods, and techniques in theatre and related disciplines. The education of teachers must include consideration of various social, cultural, and historical contexts and not be merely the accumulation of discrete skills, activities, and facts. Synthesis of often conflicting and ambiguous information, critical thinking, and a willingness to experiment and find one's own voice and style as an educator and artist are essential.

I spoke with several university faculty members about their work with preservice teachers and the role their programs play in shaping change in our field. Bob Colby (2002) and Bethany Nelson teach at Emerson College in Boston. Bob spoke about partnerships with K–12 schools and how he and Bethany have woven theory, practice, and field experiences into a teacher education program that enables students to learn and apply best practice principles.

> From the very . . . first day of class, [we] immerse [students] in some of the strategies they weren't likely to have encountered and that we think are the basis of good practice. . . . [For example,] they'll be immersed in . . . play-making experiences as a series of ongoing in-class activities and . . . we send them out to observe practicing teachers in the area doing [similar activities] with their students. . . . We've woven in story of cultures really strongly from day one. We ask them to [always] think about that in terms of their practice. . . . And they have pre-practicum experiences that are done in schools . . . with students of color. . . . We can point a student to a particular school to see a certain kind of high-level, experienced teacher doing something that they can be invited to model and be comfortable modeling. Those teachers also come in and teach seminars . . . within some of the other coursework that we offer. . . . We try to keep that partnership between the practice sites and the college as close as we can.
>
> By the end of the first year [students] realize all of the different possible ways in which the work can proceed and challenge the sort of orthodoxy of many of their own experiences. . . . [We] help them see that the Constructivist approach to education is going to help them as they shape theatre pieces [and] listen to the understandings of a group of people and build from there. . . . We try to make explicit those links between what best practices in education in general are and how that actually actively translates to the theatre classroom. . . . [When students say] "Well, I'm teaching acting. I don't know what this idea about modeling or coaching or facilitating that I read

about in education is," we . . . [deal with and] talk about [that]. We have an opportunity to effect considerable change in what's happening in the New England states. (Colby 2002)

The philosophy of teacher education at Emerson resonates with other teachers of teachers who participated in national think tanks[1] on theatre teacher education held throughout the country. Sandy Zielinski (2002) is director of theatre education at Illinois State University (ISU). ISU graduates are employed in schools throughout Illinois. Like Bob and Bethany, she and colleague Cyndee Brown have developed a program that places preservice teachers in the schools from their first year in the program. In this way they immediately apply theory to practice.

When they're freshmen they hear about student-centered practice and performance-based assessment. . . . They have to be attuned to the students from the very beginning. . . . [They learn that] although at times they can lecture, that's one method out of a hundred [they] can choose. . . . So they have to problem solve. . . . It's never static. . . . They have to attend to each student's problems, they have to attend to secondary teachers' problems, professional problems, and listen and respond from that point of view versus "This is what I want to do." . . . (Zielenski 2002)

Figure 6–1 *A teacher and her students each share stories about their heritage and culture.*

Graduate-level programs in theatre education at New York University, Arizona State University, and The University of Texas at Austin have played an enormous role in changing the practice of many of the teacher-artists I interviewed. Brianna Lindahl (2002b) and Diane Stewart (2002), whose ideas were shared earlier in this book, each spoke about their master's work at the University of Utah. They were both involved in a long-term distance-learning program for working teachers that blended study and practice in directing and theatre education. In the summers, teacher-students from around the country worked at the Sundance Festival and interacted with faculty at the university in Salt Lake City. During the school year they engaged in online coursework and applied these ideas in their own classrooms each day. University of Utah faculty traveled to observe and mentor teachers in their home schools. Dave Dynak, who heads this program, also includes undergraduate theatre education majors in work at Sundance so they "have a much more visceral, direct experience with new work development than they had had before" (2002).

I asked Dave about practices they use in their undergraduate theatre education classes that have had a direct impact on the teachers' practice when they enter the field.

> One of the strategies that has been the most powerful is . . . a one-credit course that we [require] every semester [for four semesters]. . . . It's called Theatre Forum and Practicum. . . . We discuss and explore content, but we also create [work] together. . . . We create . . . process dramas that support productions, either department productions or [our resident professional] Pioneer Theatre Company (PTC) productions.
>
> We've linked our students with PTC in a lot of ways. . . . One of the things that I [noticed when I first came here] was that [PTC] does school matinees. [I said] "How about if we create process dramas that will be taken to the schools, pre-show, [for] the students [who] come and see the shows?" . . . So our students . . . study . . . process drama . . . but at the same time they're looking at it as part of . . . creating a process drama to support *Richard the Third* . . . or . . . *View from the Bridge* or . . . *Romeo and Juliet*. . . . That has been really strong because that bridges it for [our students]. . . . When they . . . do these process dramas with kids, they [say] . . . "The kids were great. They were engaged, they cared about the work they were doing, and it was a great deal of fun." Then they sit behind the kids during the matinees to watch the kids' responses, and they always say, "It's . . . amazing how sophisticated they are about the show they're seeing." We're engaging [young people] in an exploration of the historical context of the show, exploration of the key themes of the show, . . . explorations of key moments of the show. . . . We're trying to use, somewhat, the framework of the National Standards and marrying that framework with process drama work. (Dynak 2002)

Laura McCammon (2002c) taught in the public schools in Tennessee for eighteen years prior to moving to Arizona for graduate work. She now heads the BFA in theatre education program at the University of Arizona. She and colleague Bobbie McKean teach undergraduate and graduate theatre education students and elementary education majors in a number of drama and theatre classes. Laura sees a shift in the way she is approaching teacher education.

I used to say "Before you go into your field placement, these are the things you need to find out." [Now] I ask them, "What do you need to know before you can teach this class?" They'll see it as something they've created themselves. (McCammon 2002c)

Laura and I talked about the art and craft of teaching theatre and how she inspires students' growth.

> I compare a good theatre program . . . to ice skating because a good ice skater has to have good technique . . . to do the jumps. . . . You've got to have those things in place, but you can still be artistic about it. . . . If you look at someone like Michele Kwan, she has an awful lot of joy in what she does, and that's one of the things that distinguishes her [from] the mediocre skaters and the really wonderful skaters. . . . She brings so much joy, she just draws the audience in. I think that's kind of the way teaching is. There's a lot of technique—and you've got to have the technique—but you also have to figure out how to have joy in your work. (McCammon 2002b)

At my own institution, The University of Texas at Austin, I too have thought about how to share the joy of this work with preservice teachers. I often wonder how best to position eighteen through twenty-two-year-olds—still adolescents themselves—for their work as professional theatre educators. I have found that using multiple approaches to their own comprehensive theatre education allows them to learn, apply, reflect, and develop their own practice. Class and field work engage students in investigation of practices that are learner-centered and socially responsible. Best practice principles are embedded in field experiences and course work in drama-in-education, directing young performers, theatre for young audiences, theatre-in-education, and other teaching methods. I continue to explore new models for early placement of students in the field and more extensive correlation between classroom experiences and regular interactions with professional theatre artists and educators. Community-based learning opportunities and colloquia that foster ongoing dialogue with high quality, K–12 theatre educators are areas for my further exploration.

Challenges to Change in Higher Education

There are enormous challenges to making change in theatre teacher education. In many college and university theatre departments the theatre education program is understaffed, underfunded, or marginalized. Some theatre education faculty members are still teaching theatre education as it was practiced fifty years ago. They are isolated from colleagues in education and theatre education and they may never have taught in a secondary school themselves. On many campuses, theatre departments and colleges of education rarely work together to develop best practice programs for theatre education majors. Some states only require students to take six hours in theatre prior to certification. In many communities, it is also difficult to find secondary school theatre teachers who are aware of or are utilizing best practice principles. This leaves preservice teachers no place to see these principles in action.

While a great deal has been done at the national and state levels to promote quality theatre teacher education, positive change must be implemented at the local level. As those closest to teacher education—professors of education, theatre, and theatre education—model best practice, their students will be encouraged to do the same. In this way we will be the change we hope to bring about. Figure 6–2 is an open letter to inspire and challenge our next generation of theatre educators.

Ideas for Further Reflection

Developing a Teaching Philosophy

Read "A Letter to Future Theatre Teachers" (see Figure 6–2) and then jot down some notes about what you value about theatre and about education: What can you, and the artform you practice, offer different young people in a school community? What is your role in the lives of these young people, and how does theatre empower you as an educator and your students as learners, artists, and citizens?

Now think about who your audience is for your teaching philosophy. It may be read by a principal or personnel director unfamiliar with theatre and theatre education. How can you express your vision of theatre education in such a way that these people will understand and feel your passion? Write a draft and invite

Figure 6–2 *A Letter to Future Theatre Teachers*

Dear Future Theatre Educator,

Your role as a theatre educator is to live in the intersection between art and education. It is not always an easy place to be. You are embarking on a journey of exploration, study, and development of theatre with students in your school community. This is a shared adventure, one in which students discover relationships between their lives and the lives of those who have preceded them and those who will follow them. This journey so powerfully captures aspects of the human experience that it can enable learners to better understand themselves, their fellow human beings, and their world.

But this requires a teacher. Someone who will navigate between learning and artmaking, someone who recognizes that production of plays with young people is also about development of new understandings, that art is only art when it can stir in us an understanding of beauty or the contemplation of ideas beyond mere words. This shift in understanding can cause our hearts to care about the strangers who people the world of a play and the world in which we live. That is the gift of theatre and to teach less is to deprive our students of a powerful tool through which they can grow. But it must be used skillfully and responsibly and with a clear sense of purpose.

The impact of theatre on your students may not be visible to you, but you must trust that, if taught with integrity and clarity, theatre education will enrich those whom you serve and enlarge their humanity.

You are entering a noble profession. You have the privilege of working in a dynamic artform and the joy of sharing the rich history, power, and significance of that artform with the next generation of artists and audiences. This will happen as you yourself grow as a thinker and nurturer of the human spirit as well as an artist and educator.

colleagues or other teachers to read it and give you feedback. Continue to revise your philosophy as you grow as a theatre education pioneer.

Rethinking a Theatre Teacher Education Program

Revisit the ideas explored in Chapters 1–5 and consider to what extent your college and university program models principles of best practice. In what ways can you change your curriculum, your program of study, and your relationships with colleagues on campus and in the community to bring more of these principles into the curriculum for your theatre education majors? Reach out to state and national professional theatre education organizations and individual faculty members and teachers in your area who can help you realize your vision for your program. Develop a plan of action and invite others to join you on this journey of change.

Selected Resources

There are a multitude of resources that examine aspects of the education of teachers. The following are a few for further reflection about ideas raised in this chapter.

Dooley, Cindy. 1998. "Teaching as a Two-Way Street: Discontinuities Among Metaphors, Images, and Classroom Realities." *Journal of Teacher Education* 49 (2): 97–107.

Garcia, Lorenzo. 2000. "Placing 'Diverse Voices' at the Center of Teacher Education: A Preservice Teacher's Conception of *Educacion* and Appeal to Caring." *Youth Theatre Journal* 14: 85–100.

———. 2002. "Uncovering Hidden Stories: Preservice Teachers Explore Cultural Connections." *Stage of the Art* 14 (4): 5–9.

Norris, Joe, Laura A. McCammon, and Carole S. Miller. 2000. *Learning to Teach Drama: A Case Narrative Approach*. Portsmouth, NH: Heinemann.

Scherer, Marge. "Improving the Quality of the Teaching Force: A Conversation with David C. Berliner." *Educational Leadership* 58 (8): 6–10.

Note

1. At the American Alliance for Theatre and Education (AATE) national conference in 1998, the Higher Education and High School Networks received funds from AATE for a gathering of those concerned with theatre teacher education. The planning committee, cochaired by the author and JoBeth Gonzalez, determined that, rather than a single event, this think tank would be ongoing gatherings of diverse groups of thinkers and practitioners. The intent was to probe important issues, move the field to "a new level of thinking," and, hopefully, effect change in individual and collective practice of teacher education. Think tanks have since been held in individual states and at several national conferences (Lazarus 2002).

7

Visions of Change

I began this book with my childhood desire to change the whole world. I know today that I can't do that. But *I* can change. My thinking and my practice can change. And then, in small and large ways, as I embrace change, I make a difference in the world.

A number of different visions, desires, and hopes for making a difference in our field are shared in this chapter. I begin with a small group of nationally recognized leaders in the arts and education who share their thoughts about our work, our practice, and our future. The chapter concludes with the voices of teachers and artists, who as they work day to day with secondary school students, are the shapers of change.

A Wider View of Change

Thoughts from Ben Cameron, Maxine Greene, Kent Seidel, and David O'Fallon

Over the last few years I have had the opportunity to chat with some remarkable people about the future of theatre education, talking about their own journeys as artists and educators and their sense of where theatre education is headed. I find their ideas challenging, provocative, and inspiring. Individually and together their perspectives resonate with and enlarge upon ideas about best practice already shared in this book.

Ben Cameron (2000) is a scholar, artist, and arts activist with a long history of support for theatre education. He is the executive director of Theatre Communications Group (TCG), has worked at the National Endowment for the Arts as director of the theatre programs, and has been an associate artistic director, literary manager, and freelance artist at a number of professional theatres around the country. He also has taught at several universities and is currently an adjunct faculty member at Columbia University. Ben and I talked about how he was introduced to theatre.

> You're going to find a fierce commitment [to theatre education], especially from people who grew up in non-urban areas, who wouldn't have encountered theatre in any other context. . . . Had there not been the Junior League coming in and doing a sort of hands-on arts program with us, I would have gone through the gamut without ever knowing what theatre was. . . . For a lot of us . . . that . . . was the way we got introduced to theatre and we're appreciative of that. (2000)

Ben also talked about theatre participation as a powerful tool for enlarging the social development of young people.

> There's . . . one study that demonstrates that kids that work[ed] in theatre—not in the arts, but in theatre specifically—are forty percent . . . less likely to tolerate racist behavior than kids who are not participating in the theatre. And the kids that participated in theatre—*participated* in theatre—not as witness[es] . . . work better across racial lines than any other group. . . . The role for us is [to value] the inherent social dimensions . . . that . . . creative hands-on experience offers us. (2000)

Ben speaks passionately about the value of theatre and theatre education to our children and our country.

> It's so ironic to me that there's such public support for athletics which clearly has a great ability for teamwork and a kind of physical health. But I would argue that . . . theatre has a spiritual health connection. It emphasizes . . . cooperation and teamwork. And frankly . . . I can't think of the actor who has broken a kneecap of a rival or slashed somebody with a hockey stick or been brought in on assault charges. . . . By reinforcing the arts . . . we can get a lot of the same benefits of athletics for a lot of different kids without a lot of the negatives. We've got a big, uphill battle about proving this to people, but I think that's our part.
>
> I think . . . that we lack . . . at present, both the research that's convincing and the arguments that stick with the people that matter. . . . If the evidence we've got is not convincing, then we don't have the right arguments; we don't have the right evidence. . . . When Kennedy stood up in the early sixties and said: "Everybody's going to have to take a sport and gym's going to be compulsory for everybody" . . . the argument was for your physical well-being and the long-term sake of the country. You had to engage in this activity . . . no ifs, ands, or buts. It seems to me we're at that nascent point where we need to be able to say, for the spiritual health of this country, "You will engage in the arts, no ifs, ands . . . or buts." (2000)

In a 2001 keynote address, Ben stressed the importance of talking in a "listener-targeted way" about the value of what we do.

It is critical that we not abandon this fight.
—Ben Cameron

For your local board of education, the value of the arts is that kids who work in the arts perform eighty points higher on the SATs than kids who don't. . . . And we have the tests to prove it. For the principals in your school systems, the value of the arts is that kids who work in after-school arts programs show decreasing disciplinary infractions than kids who don't. For parents it is the reams of studies . . . that prove that kids who work in the arts have a greater complexity in thinking, greater tolerance for ambiguity, greater self-esteem, greater sense of self. . . . For people concerned about community building . . . the reason the arts and theatre is important is because high-school seniors who work in theatre are forty percent less likely to tolerate racist behavior than kids who never created a piece of theatre. Clarity on our values is essential to our survival. (Cameron 2001, 22)

Maxine Greene (2000) is a professor of education and philosophy (emerita) at Columbia University where she founded the Center for the Arts, Social Imagination, and Education. Maxine teaches at the Lincoln Center for the Arts and speaks at conferences and events throughout the country. She has written extensively on the arts, aesthetic education, and social change. I asked about her current work and what issues she was thinking about in terms of arts education. Among the topics we discussed, Maxine spoke about how we inadvertently alienate young people in school by making assumptions about them.

[An organization] hired a group from the Ivory Coast . . . [to perform] for the kids in Buffalo. I said "What . . . do black kids in Buffalo know about the Ivory Coast . . . just because [they're] the same color? These kids are interested in rap." . . . I think it's a kind of racism sometimes to push these kids into African stuff. I don't want to have Jewish literature [just because I come from a Jewish tradition].

Maxine's desire is to make her work as a teacher inviting and inclusive. She says, "When I teach . . . I want to say, 'Come in. It's exciting.' . . . I don't want to say, 'I'm transmitting this. You have to have it if you're going to make it.' I want to say, 'This is an exciting life.'"

Maxine also talked about how essential it is that students stay engaged and alive in school and how central the arts can be to realizing that goal.

Children are in search of meaning. They're not empty. . . . I . . . talk a lot about being alive because the schools don't do anything about that. . . . Sometimes the schools are for forgetting . . . the perceived world, the imagined world. . . . I write about wide awakeness. I want to think about classrooms that are dialogues. It's very important for teachers to know how many voices are silenced and what you do to [not let that happen]. . . . [They have] to . . . understand . . . what's happening in the culture [and] about the relation between popular culture and what we're doing in the arts. . . . How do I attend to the students' world and communicate what I think is valuable? And how do I say, "What do you love?" I think, like Marcusse said, "Art doesn't change the world. It can change the people who might change the world." (Greene 2000)

In her book *Releasing the Imagination*, Maxine pushes us to move beyond the traditions of American education and to explore with children the possibilities of our collective human experience.

> To help the diverse students we know articulate their stories isn't only to help them pursue the meaning of their lives—to find out *how* things are happening and to keep posing questions about the why. It is to move them . . . to reach out for the proficiencies and capacities, the craft required to be fully participant in this society, and to do so without losing the consciousness of who they are. (Greene 1995, 165)

Kent Seidel (2002) has a long-term connection to theatre education. He is a faculty member both in the Educational Administration Program and in the Urban Educational Leadership Cultural Program at the University of Cincinnati. He also is the executive director of the Alliance for Curriculum Reform. Before this, Kent was program director for the Lexington Council for the Arts and headed the Educational Theatre Association, the teacher services branch of the International Thespian Society. He talked with me about changes occurring as theatre programs branch out to embrace larger social issues and as teachers reach out to people outside of the arts.

> I think we're starting to see teachers thinking about theatre education in a little broader sense than [just] putting on the senior play. And I really believe that that has started to snowball. . . . I'm not sure theatre is yet connecting very well with the curriculum as a whole, although I think we are seeing a lot more evidence [of that].
>
> I really think one of the things we can do is . . . to make arts experiences a part of administrator preparation. . . . So we've got folks at the very top of each school building who have had some [arts] experiences . . . [so] they understand how and why it can be important in the lives of their kids and their community. (Seidel 2002)

I asked Kent to share ways in which the work can stay vital and powerful for teachers themselves. He envisions

> teachers as learners . . . participating as audiences and performers . . . on an ongoing, regular basis to keep their learning going and to keep their excitement about what they're doing. [Teachers can] find new ideas by working with artists. . . . I'd like to see them be comfortable with the arts side of what we do. . . . To venture out of the stage . . . [and] have a . . . broad understanding of . . . [the] importance of theatre and performing arts in the world of human beings. Not just a dry, historical view, but really to understand all that socially responsible stuff.
>
> Everybody ought to have what this artform offers as part of their toolbox. . . . It's not that they can all act or recite some Shakespeare, but that they have at their disposal these things that for many thousands of years have been part of the human experience. I think that requires [preparing] novice teachers much differently as far as . . . kinds of course work . . . experiences, and opportunities to be reflective.

I think our theatre teachers really are . . . in a position in the [school] to . . . be . . . instructional . . . and . . . inspirational to their colleagues. When I see . . . integrated arts projects take off . . . in the schools . . . [what] I see is a commonality, a collaboration happen. . . . Those folks who have . . . artistic skills are able to bring [them] to their other colleagues in the school and take a leadership role. And together all of them find things that are not just exciting for the kids, but also exciting for all subject teachers. I think arts teachers have a particular advantage to take that exciting leadership role in transforming the school. (Seidel 2002)

In Chapter 1 I shared some of David O'Fallon's concerns about our public schools. I asked him to talk with me also about changes he would like to see in our field. He spoke about how teachers and artists are stewards of the inner wilderness and how "we need to nurture [the] inner wilderness, inner spirit, inner soul . . . and take time to do that" (2002). To that end, David would like to see professional development programs for teachers and school personnel that call for and support this kind of nurturing.

David also spoke of his wish for teachers to be

working across multiple forms and thinking [about] connections and relationships. . . . Committing . . . to a community . . . so that other people hold us accountable in healthy ways for what we do. There's still a little bit of, "we're artists, and you should understand us" rather than . . . "I'm committing myself to building community." (2000)

David's closing thought is a wish for teacher-artists for "continual affirmation and support for what they do because it is not valuable now, but increasingly valuable" (2002).

Pioneers and Change Makers

When I think about the value of theatre education, as evidenced by the range of work described in this book, I forget where the rest of our field is for a moment and really believe best practice is widespread. In reality, best practice in theatre education today is just a glimpse of *what could be*. This practice exists like those fireflies in the night, visible only in small, elusive glimmers. This book has gathered some fireflies to illumine our thinking and light our paths. I have written for the pioneer, the one who, as Margaret Wheatley (1994) says, is calling "Land ho" on desire, faith, and intuition. Those already on their journey have found in these pages reassurance that what they are doing with students is effective, though not always visible or valued. Others have found courage and encouragement to embrace change and embark on a new path. I hope this book will create a positive epidemic of change and spread it to other pioneers for the benefit of our children and communities.

I leave you with the hopes and desires of our most precious resource, our theatre teachers, teaching artists, and future teachers. In their day to day work with secondary-school students they are creating the signs of change leading our field in new directors.

Interviewees were all invited to share something they are learning in their practice, a wish, or piece of advice that might ensure a vibrant future for secondary school theatre education. Here are but a few of their comments.

A wish . . . would be that [teachers and students] could be involved in a production where they can see love dissolving difference or they can see what they've done has built a bond or . . . an understanding. . . . That it opened the door to somebody else. A door to possibilities.

—Tara Affolter, Teacher

I am learning that learning is never over—that embracing my ignorance as a challenge to learn more will benefit not only me but my students.

—Preservice teacher

I really believe as educators you need to take time to . . . [take a] class. . . . You have to service your artistic soul. If all you're doing is being the director and producer of your theatre company you're not getting to service your own artistic needs . . . [which] . . . inspire you. . . . If I have any [legacy] . . . it [would be] trying to create a network, a family of theatre teachers, bringing theatre teachers together so they don't feel so isolated in their field.

—Susan Morrell, Teacher

Invite people into your drama process to see [it]. . . . If the math teacher is not sure of what drama is and it is a foreign concept, then when cuts come and when . . . the opportunity to expand the program comes, you may not have those voices to [help you]. Everybody has been in somebody's math class, probably. Everybody has probably been in somebody's reading class. But throughout the country, everybody has not always been in a drama class—not the play experience—but a drama class. So it's hard for other people to value what they don't necessarily understand.

—Gloria Bond Clunie, Teacher and Playwright

I wish someone would have told me that this job would be not only the best I've ever had, but also the most challenging . . . often in one day!

—Preservice teacher

All new teachers must remember that they are usually following in someone else's footsteps. That [former teacher] may have been brilliant, or they may have been awful, but those kids are in the program, at least in part, because of who was there last year. . . . You will not win them all over the first, or even the second year. . . . The time will come when you are recognized for who you are and what you bring and not for who you aren't and what is missing.

—Sarah Kent, Teacher

I think the fact that we . . . have the National Standards . . . is a really good sign. We . . . need to address implementation. . . . Other curriculum areas have revised the National Standards already. That hasn't even begun in our field. We just went "Yay! Thank God!" and never turned back.

—Jeffrey Leptak-Moreau, Educational Theatre Association

I constantly remind myself that if the students aren't listening, it doesn't matter what I say.

—Roxanne Schroeder-Arce, Teacher

A wish for a novice teacher. . . . Be aware that you're going be faced with reality. . . . You'll be idealistic. . . . You have to stay that way and it will help you get through the reality of . . . budget and curriculum and buildings and things like that. [A wish for] a veteran teacher . . . look back and find why you were idealistic in the first place, as a new teacher.

—Kent Sorensen, Teacher

Seek out people who are doing it differently [than you]. . . . Look at your own work and [ask] "What's really strong about it? What's weak about it? What could I do differently? What could I change? Am I still taking risks artistically or educationally?" . . . And . . . look at some of the current research in education and how you might apply that to theatre.

—Karen Kay Husted, Consultant

I am learning that teaching is really about students first and subject matter second.

—Preservice teacher

I have a theme that we deal with called "Each one reach one. Each one teach one. Each one pull one into the sun." It's a Malcolm X quote. [I tell students] "You have a responsibility that once you have attained a gift, to pass it on to your community." . . . So they tour [to nearby elementary schools] and . . . they learn how to teach . . . or . . . we help them with their play . . . "What is education for and about?" . . . I ask kids that all the time and try to get them to want to learn, to be excited about learning, to be positive about themselves.

—Jan Mandell, Teacher

We were talking over lunch, and several of the kids said [one of our teaching artists] was their favorite teacher. I said "Why?" And they said "Because she's hard but she's fun, and it's clear she's a real actress herself."

—Abbey Adams, People's Light and Theatre Company

One of the most exciting parts about teaching theatre is that there's always a passion there. In every semester there'll be a new group of kids . . . who see theatre not as "I'm going to do this the rest of my life," but "I understand what theatre is, and it will always be a part of what I want. . . . I will go to the theatre or be in community theatre or do theatre . . . because it is so important in our culture—in our lives—and it's important [as] a place for our stories to be told." . . . [That's] when a student really begins to discover their talent and ability to contribute to a larger community.

—John Heinemann, Teacher

Individually and collectively we indeed are "on the verge." I look forward to meeting you on the path. Journey on!

Figure 7–1   *A teacher shares her vision of theatre with the next generation.*

WORKS CITED

Adams, Abigail. 2002. Interview with the author. Tape recording. 16 July.

Affolter, Tara. 2002. Telephone interview with the author. Tape recording. 28 June.

Alexander, Deb. 1999. A Middle School Theatre Curriculum Model. Master's Thesis. The University of Texas at Austin.

———. 2002. Interview with the author. Tape recording. 13 February.

Barnes, Dave. 1999. Oswego High School Theatre Handbook. Oswego, IL: Oswego High School.

———. 2002. Interview with the author. Tape recording. 2 August.

Barnes, Donna. 2002. Interview with the author. Tape recording. 2 August.

Bartow, Arthur. 1988. *The Director's Voice*. New York: Theatre Communications Group.

Berghammer, Gretta. 2002. Telephone interview with the author. Tape recording. 6 May.

Bishop, Nancy. 1992. "Are Your Classes Gender Fair?." *Teaching Theatre* 4 (1): 1–2, 7–10.

Bloom, Michael. 2001. *Thinking Like a Director*. New York: Faber and Faber.

Boal, Augusto. 1985. *Theatre of the Oppressed*. Trans. Charles A. and Maria-Odilia Leal McBride. New York: Theatre Communications Group.

———. 1994. *Games for Actors and Non-Actors*. Trans. Adrian Jackson. London: Routledge.

Bogart, Anne. 2001. *A Director Prepares*. New York: Routledge.

Bogart, Steve. 2003a. Telephone interview with the author. Tape recording. 3 July.

———. 2003b. "Conflict with Authority." Instructional materials shared with the author.

Brockett, Oscar G. 1985. "Drama: A Way of Knowing." *Theatre Education: Mandate for Tomorrow*. Louisville, KY: Anchorage Press and the Children's Theatre Foundation.

Burtaine, Amy. 2003a. Interview with the author. 24 June.

———. 2003b. Pre-thesis organizational draft. The University of Texas in Austin.

———. 2003c. "Searching for 'Socially Responsible Theatre Practice (SRTP)': A Journey." Pre-thesis paper. The University of Texas in Austin.

Byrne-Jiménez, Mónica. 1992. Los Solos: The education and experience of Latino children. Master's thesis. The University of Michigan, Ann Arbor.

Cain, Carol. 2003. Telephone interview with the author. Tape recording. 19 July.

Cameron, Ben. 2000. Interview with the author. Tape recording. 13 March.

———. 2001. "Keynote Address." *TYA Today* 15 (2): 19, 22.

Casey, Autumn Samsula. 2003. Interview with the author. Tape recording. 24 January.

Chapman, Jennifer. 2000. "Female Impersonations: Young Performers and the Crises of Adolescence." *Youth Theatre Journal* 14: 123–131.

———. 2002. Telephone interview with the author. Tape recording. 25 April.

Chapman, Jennifer, Heather Sykes, and Anne Swedberg. 2003. "Wearing the Secret Out: Performing Stories of Sexual Identities." *Youth Theatre Journal* 17: 27–37.

Clunie, Gloria Bond. 2002. Interview with the author. Tape recording. 5 August.

Colby, Bob. 2002. Interview with the author. Tape recording. 29 July.

Consortium of National Arts Education Associations. 1994 *National Standard for Arts Education*. Reston, VA: Consortium of National Arts Education Associations.

———. 2002. *Authentic Connections: Interdisciplinary Work in the Arts*. Reston, VA: Consortium of National Arts Education Associations.

Cooperrider, David L., and Diana Whitney. 1999. *Appreciative Inquiry*. San Francisco: Berrett-Koehler Communications.

Cooperrider, David. L., Peter F. Sorensen, Jr., Diana Whitney, and T. F. Yaeger, eds. 2000. *Appreciative Inquiry: Rethinking Human Organization Toward a Positive Theory of Change*. Champaign, IL: Stripes Publishing.

Cougle, Bryar. 2002. Telephone interview with the author. Tape recording. 30 May.

Cox, Barbara. 2002. Interview with the author. Tape recording. 29 July.

DeWinter, Micha. 1997. *Children as Fellow Citizens: Participation and Commitment*. New York: Radcliff Medical Press.

DiMartino, Sandra. 2003. Telephone interview with the author. Tape recording. 22 June.

diRende, Susan. 1996. Facsimile letter to the author. 30 October.

———. 2002. Telephone interview with the author. Tape recording. 21 June.

Dixon, Michael Bigelow, and Joel A. Smith, eds. 1995. *Anne Bogart Viewpoints*. Lyme, NH: Smith and Kraus.

Dynak, Dave. 2002. Telephone interview with the author. Tape recording. 1 July.

Eaton, Gillian. 2001. Interview with the author. Tape recording. 23 February.

Ewing, Jason. 2002. Telephone interview with the author. Tape recording. May 22.

Flint Community Schools. 1995. *Profile of Student Life, Research and Testing.* Flint, MI: Flint Community Schools.

Flint Youth Theatre. 2001. *Fact Sheet: Flint Youth Theatre Animating Democracy Initiative.* 10 January.

Freire, Paulo. 1996. *Pedagogy of the Oppressed.* New York: The Continuum Publishing Company.

Garbarino, James. 1999. *Lost Boys.* New York: Free Press.

Garcia, Lorenzo. 1997. "Drama, Theatre, and the Infusion of Multiethnic Content: An Exploratory Study." *Youth Theatre Journal* 11: 88–101.

———. 1998a. "Multiculturism, Diversity, and AATE?" *Stage of the Art* 9 (7): 3.

———. 1998b. "Learning In and Through Dialogue." *Stage of the Art* 9 (6): 3.

Garcia, Rick. 2002. Interview with the author. Tape recording. 12 February.

Giffin, Holly. 1999. "Coda Essay." *Stage of the Art* 11 (1): 34.

Gonzalez, JoBeth. 1999. "Beyond the Boundaries of Tradition: Cultural Treasures in a High School Theatre Arts Program." *Stage of the Art* (10) 3: 14.

———. 2002a. "From Page to Stage to Teenager: Problematizing 'Transformation' in Theatre for and with Adolescents." *Stage of the Art* 14 (3): 17–21.

———. 2002b. Interview with the author. Tape recording. 13 February.

———. 2003. Email to the author. 27 May.

Goodrich, Frances, and Albert Hackett. 1958. *The Diary of Anne Frank.* New York: Dramatist Play Service.

Goodrich, Frances, Albert Hackett, and Wendy Ann Kesselman. 2000. *The Diary of Anne Frank.* Updated. New York: Dramatist Play Service.

Gotuaco, Fursey. 2002. Interview with the author. Tape recording. 20 February.

Grady, Sharon. 2000. *Drama and Diversity.* Portsmouth, NH: Heinemann.

Greene, Maxine. 1995. *Releasing the Imagination: Essays on Education, the Arts, and Social Change.* San Francisco: Jossey-Bass.

———. 2000. Interview with the author. Tape recording. 14 March.

Griffith, Chris. 2002a. *News from the Playground.* 10 (Summer).

———. 2002b. Telephone interview with the author. Tape recording. 28 July.

Hall, Brian. 1999. Instructional materials shared with the author.

———. 2003a. Email to the author. 22 June.

———. 2003b. Email to the author. 21 June.

———. 2003c. Email to the author. 21 March.

Hansen, Bill. 2002. Interview with the author. Tape recording. 6 August.

———. 2003. "The Spot." Email to the author. 7 July.

Heathcote, Dorothy, and Gavin Bolton. 1995. *Drama for Learning: Dorothy Heathcote's Mantle of the Expert*. Portsmouth, NH: Heinemann.

Heinemann, John. 2002. Telephone interview with the author. Tape recording. 11 June.

Herring, J. Daniel. 2002. Telephone interview with the author. Tape recording. 24 May.

Hock, Dee. 1999. *Birth of the Chaordic Age*. San Francisco: Berrett-Koehler Publishers.

Interstate New Teacher Assessment and Support Consortium (INTASC) Arts Education Committee. 2002. *Model Standards for Licensing Classroom Teachers and Specialists in the Arts*. Draft for Comments. Washington, DC: Council of Chief State School Officers.

Jallings, Rebecca. 2002. Personal interview with the author. Tape recordings. 6 August.

Johns, Patsy Koch. 2002. Telephone interview with the author. Tape recording. 19 June.

———. 2003. Email to the author. 25 October.

Johnson, Julie. 2003. Email to the author. 15 July.

Jones, Steven. 2002. Interview with the author. Tape recording. 4 May.

Kelin, Daniel. 2001. Interview with the author. Tape recording. 1 August.

Kent, Sarah. 2003. Email to the author. 31 August.

Kindlon, Daniel J., and Michael Thompson. 2000. *Raising Cain: Protecting the Emotional Life of Boys*. New York: Ballantine.

Knighton, Aline. 2003. Email to the author. 1 July.

Korza, Pam. 2001a. Email correspondence to the author. 9 February.

———. 2001a. Notes from welcome to the Flint study circles. Unpublished. 22 February.

Labonski, Valerie Roberts. 2002. Telephone interview with author. Tape recording. 12 October.

Ladson-Billings, Gloria. 1994. *The Dreamkeepers: Successful Teachers of African American Children*. San Francisco: Jossey-Bass.

Lamb, Gregory, M. 2003. "Some Serious Child's Play." *The Christian Science Monitor* (17 October): 13, 20.

Lang, Linda, L. 2002. "'Whose Play Is it Anyhow?' When Drama Teachers Journey into Collective Creation." *Youth Theatre Journal* 16: 48–62.

Larson, Jeanette. 2003. Review of *With Their Eyes: September 11th—View from a High School at Ground Zero*. Edited by Annie Thoms. Austin, TX: Austin American Statesman.

Lazarus, Joan. 1986. "Theatre Survey." *Southern Theatre* XXVII (3) 6–7.

———. 2000. "On the Verge: Promise or Peril for Theatre Education in the Next One Hundred Years." *Arts Education Policy Review* Nov/Dec 101 (2).

———. 2001. "Theatre as Civic Dialogue: Questions and Considerations Raised by Flint Youth Theatre's Animating Democracy Through the Arts Project." *TYA Today* 15 (2): 24–27.

———. 2002. "Rethinking Theatre Teacher Education: A National Think Tank for Change-Makers." *Stage of the Art* 14 (3): 5–6.

Lerman, Liz, and John Borstel. 2003. *Liz Lerman's Critical Response Process*. Takoma Park, MD: Liz Lerman Dance Exchange.

Lindahl, Brianna. 2002a. Instructional materials shared with the author.

———. 2002b. Telephone interview with the author. Tape recording. 22 July.

Lutringer, Jenny. 2002a. Interview with the author. 20 February.

———. 2002b. Interview with the author. Tape recording. 22 July.

———. 2003a. Email to the author. 5 April.

———. 2003b. Email to the author. 22 July.

———. 2003c. The Open Theatre instructional materials shared with the author.

MacDonald, George. 1969. *The Light Princess* New York: Farrar, Straus and Giroux.

Mandell, Jan. 2002. Interview with the author. Tape recording. 30 July.

Markowitz, Elaine. 2003. "A teen improves with 'Crime and Punishment.'" *The Christian Science Monitor* (18 June).

McCammon, Laura. 2002a. "Deconstructing Youthland." *Stage of the Art* (14) 3: 7–11.

———. 2002b. Telephone interview with the author. Tape recording. 3 June.

———. 2002c. Email to the author. 27 August.

McLauchlan, Debra. 2001. "Collaborative Creativity in a High School Drama Class." *Youth Theatre Journal* 15: 42–58.

McNally, Gillian. 2002a. Empowering Ophelia: Feminist theater principles in devising and directing youth theater. Master's thesis. The University of Texas at Austin.

———. 2002b. Email to the author. 30 June.

Metz, Allison Manville. 2002. Recognizing Relationships: Avant-garde Theatre and Marginalized Youth. Master's thesis. The University of Texas at Austin.

Metz, Allison Manville, and Gillian McNally. 2001. "Reassuming Assumptions: Pedagogy for Gender Fair Classrooms Using Creative Drama." *Stage of the Art* 14 (1).

Morrell, Susan. 2002. Telephone interview with the author. Tape recording. 12 July.

Neelands, Jonothan, and Tony Goode. 2000. *Structuring Drama Work*. New York: Cambridge University Press.

Nelson, Bethany, Robert Colby, and Marisa McIlrath. 2001. "'Having Their Say: The Effects of Using Role with an Urban Middle School Class." *Youth Theatre Journal* 15: 59–69.

O'Fallon, David. 2002. Telephone interview with the author. Tape recording. 28 May.

O'Neill, Cecily. 1995. *Drama Worlds: A Framework for Process Drama*. Portsmouth, NH: Heinemann.

Orenstein, Peggy. 1994. *School Girls: Young Women, Self-Esteem, and the Confidence Gap*. New York: Doubleday.

Overmyer, Eric. 1993. "On the Verge (or The Geography of Yearning)." In *Eric Overmyer: Collected Plays*. Newbury, VT: Smith and Kraus.

Peterson, Kathryn. 2002. Lesson plan shared with the author.

Peterson, Tory. 2002. Interview with the author. Tape recording. 29 July.

Pipher, Mary. 1994. *Reviving Ophelia: Saving the Selves of Adolescent Girls*. New York: Ballatine Books.

Pollack, William. 1998. *Real Boys: Rescuing Our Sons from the Myth of Boyhood*. New York: Random House.

———. 2000. *Real Boys' Voices*. New York: Random House.

Postman, Neil. 1990. "The Re-enchantment of Learning." *Youth Theatre Journal* 5 (2): 6.

Remer, Jane. 1990. *Changing Schools through the Arts: How to Build on the Power of an Idea*. New York: American Council for the Arts.

Richter, Hans Peter. 1987. *Friedrich*. New York: Holt, Reinhart, and Winston.

Rohd, Michael. 1998. *Theatre for Community, Conflict, and Dialogue*. Portsmouth, NH: Heinemann.

Rowling, J. K. 2000. *Harry Potter and the Goblet of Fire*. New York: Scholastic.

Ryan, Tammy. 2000. *The Music Lesson*. Unpublished script. Available through Rosenstone/Wender Agency, New York.

Saldaña, Johnny. 1991. "Drama Theatre and Hispanic Youth: Interviews with Selected Teachers and Artists." *Youth Theatre Journal* 5 (4): 3–8.

Scarborough, Sue. 2003. Telephone interview with the author. Tape recording. 28 September.

Schloman, Rebecca. 2004. Theatre in the Peer Mentorship Classroom: A High School Arts Integration Model. Master's thesis. The University of Texas at Austin.

Schroeder-Arce, Roxanne. 2002a. "Walking on Ice." *Stage of the Art* 14 (3): 22–24.

———. 2002b. Interview with the author. Tape recording. 12 February.

Seidel, Kent. 2002. Telephone interview with the author. Tape recording. 7 June.

Serleth, Laurel. 2002. Interview with the author. Tape recording. 2 August.

Shippey, Kim. 1999. "Arguing on the Side of Good." *The Christian Science Sentinel* 8 (November): 18–20.

Sizer, Theodore. R., and Nancy Faust Sizer. 1999. *The Students Are Watching: Schools and the Moral Contract*. Boston: Beacon Press.

Smith, Jerry. 2002. Telephone interview with the author. Tape recording. 1 June.

Smith, J. Lea, and J. Daniel Herring. 2001. *Dramatic Literacy: Using Drama and Literature to Teach Middle-Level Content*. Portsmouth, NH: Heinemann.

Spolin, Viola. 1983. *Improvisation for the Theatre*. Evanston, IL: Northwestern University Press.

Staley, Betty. 1988. *Between Form and Freedom: A Practical Guide for the Teenage Years*. Lansdown, Stroud, UK: Hawthorn Press.

Stanfield, Holly. 2002. Interview with the author. Tape recording. 3 August.

Stewart, Diane. 1999. Shakespeare Unit Plan for Dr. Dave Dynak. University of Utah. November.

———. 2002. Interview with the author. Tape recording. 22 July.

———. 2003. Email correspondence with the author. 5 September.

Still, James. 2003. Conversation with the author and students in Issues and Practices in Youth Theatre. The University of Texas at Austin. 7 March.

Tarlington, Carole, and Wendy Michaels. 1995. *Buidling Plays*. Portsmouth, NH: Heinemann.

Valenta, Misty. 2002. Lesson plan created for Creative Drama I class. The University of Texas at Austin. Summer session.

Vine, Chris. 2000. Personal interview with the author. Tape recording. 14 March.

Ward, William. 2001a. Interview with the author. Tape recording. 23 February.

———. 2001b. . . . *My Soul to Take*. Unpublished play.

Wheatley, Margaret. 1994. *Leadership and the New Science: Learning about Organization from an Orderly Universe*. San Francisco: Berret-Koehler Publishers.

Wheetley, Kim. 2002. Telephone interview with the author. Tape recording. 4 May.

Wheetley, Kim, and Southeast Center for Education in the Arts. 1996. *Discipline-Based Theatre Education: A Conceptual Framework for Teaching and Learning Theatre*. Chattanooga, TN: Southeast Center for Education in the Arts, The University of Tennessee at Chattanooga.

———. 2003. Transforming Education Through the Arts Challenge. www.utc.edu/SCEA/Intro_TETAC_Report.pdf.

White, Helen. 2000. Personal interviews with the author. Tape recording. 14 March.

White, Helen, and Chris Vine. 2001."From the Streets to Academia . . . And Back Again: Youth Theatre, Arts Training, and the Building of Community. *Stage of the Art* 12 (2): 5–11.

Wilkinson, Nancy. 2002. Telephone interview with the author. Tape recording. 18 July.

Wood, Sue. 2001. Interview with the author. Tape recording. 24 February.

Zemelman, Steven, Harvey Daniels, and Arthur Hyde. 1998. *Best Practice: New Standards for Teaching and Learning in America's Schools*. Portsmouth, NH, Heinemann.

Zielinski, Sandy. 2002. Interview with the author. Tape recording. 5 August.

INDEX